Monica,
You are going to change
the world!
Marietta Hole

COACHING for SUCCESS

Table of Contents

A Message from the Publisher

L et's face it—there are times when even the best of us find ourselves in a rut. It seems that we are doing the same old things in the same old way and we feel that the excitement has gone out of our career.

This is when we need to stop and do some serious looking around for a good business coach. The very best way to do this, in my opinion, is to read about what some of the best business coaches have to say about what they do and how they do it. Between the covers of this book, *Coaching for Success,* you will find some of the best and brightest business coaches sharing what they know about this important topic.

This book is your golden opportunity to discover what they know and how to apply it to your business and personal life. I think you will agree with me that the interviews in this book will give you an insider's look at how to build a better life. I really enjoyed talking with these people and I learned a lot from them. I think you will too.

David Wright, President
International Speakers Network & Insight Publishing

Chapter 1

Annetta Wilson

DAVID WRIGHT (WRIGHT)

Today we're talking to Annetta Wilson. She is a Certified Professional Behavioral Analyst and Certified Trainer. She specializes in presentation and communication skills coaching and media training. Annetta coaches on-air journalists at CNN, has coached for Walt Disney World's Ambassador Program and conducted trainings for Charles Schwab and Mitsubishi Power Systems Americas, Inc., among others. She was national emcee for Office Depot's Success Strategies Conference for Businesswomen in six U.S. cities. She is a former television news anchor, reporter, talk show host and writer. Annetta is a member of the International Association of Coaching. Get her free report: "Three of the Biggest Mistakes People Make in Public Speaking!" on her Website, www.YourCoachForSuccess.com. Annetta, welcome to *Coaching for Success*.

ANNETTA WILSON (WILSON)

Thank you, David. It's a pleasure to talk to you.

WRIGHT

So what is an elevator speech?

WILSON

An elevator speech, briefly, is what you say to someone if you are in an elevator from perhaps the 5th floor to the 1st floor that gives them a snapshot of who you are and what you do.

WRIGHT

Just a first impression speech, huh?

WILSON

Yes.

WRIGHT

So why would anyone need an elevator speech?

WILSON

There are times when we have to explain our gifts and talents to the world. There are also times when we want people to pay us for those gifts and talents. There are people who need what we're good at doing. If they don't know who we are and what we offer, we can't help them. So, the elevator speech is a way of letting the world know who you are and how you can help them.

WRIGHT

So, if you're an expert, shouldn't talking about what you do come naturally?

WILSON

That's one of the biggest misconceptions of all. You can be a real pro at what you do, the best in fact, but talking about what you do is an entirely different skill set. Have you seen people who are geniuses, but when they have to give a speech or talk to someone about their work, it's as if they're speaking a foreign language? It's almost as if they don't know that there are other people in the room or how to connect with them. Then you end up saying, "I thought he was the top expert or I thought she was the best at this. They can't put two sentences together!" Very often, people will falsely judge your ability based on how you communicate. Then they decide that you're not good at what you do, and that's so unfair.

WRIGHT

So, what are some of the biggest mistakes that people make when giving their elevator speeches?

WILSON

They become what I call 'feature creatures'. They talk about the 'features' of what they offer, or the 'features' of their business as opposed to the benefits. We all listen to the same radio station, WII-FM: What's In It For Me? What we're really listening for is the answer to, "What does that mean to me?" "How am I going to benefit?" "How is this going to make my life easier, better, etc.?" So, instead of talking about how we help people, we tell them how long we've been in business, how big our company is, what our credentials are and who our clients are. None of which they care about until they know what we can do for them.

WRIGHT

So, how do you know what to put in your elevator speech?

WILSON

I always ask my clients, "What problems do you solve?" We start there. People want to know that you can fix whatever ails them. If you can talk to me about a problem I have and your ability to come to my rescue, get rid of the problem and ease whatever pain I'm in, I'm all ears. The elevator speech should focus on your problem solving abilities.

WRIGHT

That's very interesting.

WILSON

For instance, if I run a company and my company is constantly in the red, and I meet someone who has expertise in the financial arena, I'm not really interested in how many letters in the alphabet follow their last name. I want to know what results they've gotten for other people. Have they been able to use their skills, talents and abilities in a similar situation and help someone else who was in my situation turn things around? That's what I want to know. Once they can convince me of that, then I'll ask them about their credentials.

WRIGHT

So what's your elevator speech?

WILSON

My short elevator speech is, "I help people put their best foot forward, not in their mouth!" Usually when people ask me what I do, and I say I help people keep their foot out of their mouth, they do exactly what you're doing now, they laugh. Because they'll remember a time when they HAVE put their foot in their mouth or they've seen someone else do it. Or, they'll say, "Where have you been all my life?" Or, they'll say, "You must be really busy!"

I actually have a couple of elevator speeches and I suggest that for my clients as well. Humor, which is my preferred method, opens a lot of doors; it brings a lot of barriers down. So, that one is my favorite, but I'll also say, "You know how you have to sometimes speak in front of people and everyone's staring at you and your throat closes up and your mouth feels like it's stuffed with cotton and you've just forgotten everything you were going to say and you wish there was a hole in the floor that you could crawl into? I help you never feel that way again."

I address the problem and then I come in and say I can solve it. Or I'll say, "I help you talk about what you do with the same level of expertise that you actually DO what you do." I have more than one elevator speech, depending on the environment and the audience.

WRIGHT

You say that WHAT you're saying is not as important as HOW you're saying it. Can you explain that for our readers?

WILSON

Yes. This is based on the work of UCLA professor, Dr. Albert Mehrabian. His research is the generally accepted formula for the industry: 55% of our communication is non-verbal, 38% is tone of voice and the pace at which we speak. The content, what we actually say, is only 7%. So, if over half of your communication is what you're NOT saying, then your body language enters the room long before your voice does. People will buy your passion long before they will buy your product or service. Do you know the actor/comedian Ben Stein? If you are very dry, flat and monotone like Ben Stein, and you say, "I am the greatest speech coach in the entire world and I'm so excited to work with you", and you're not moving a muscle or smiling, no one is buying it. On the other hand, saying, "I am SO excited to turn you into a powerhouse speaker!" combined with movement and energy, is magnetic. The tone of your voice, the inflection and the energy behind it, usually go hand in hand with your body actually DOING something. Gestures, a smile, a pause or moving, make a huge difference. How you say something is much more important than what you say. It's like saying, 'I love you' to someone while you're reading the paper and your mind is a million miles away, as opposed to taking his or her face in both your hands, looking him or her in the eyes and saying very slowly, "I love you". The words really don't matter; it's what you're doing to get them out that's more important.

WRIGHT

So, what's the value of emotion when you're communicating?

WILSON

Well, if you're talking to me and you're excited, I'm much more likely to pay attention to you and to keep my attention riveted on you. I use the example of a child. It is extremely difficult to ignore an excited child. Think about it. Think about Christmas morning, birthday parties, think about any event where children are celebrating. It's hypnotic to watch them. It warms our hearts. It lets our defenses down when we see that pure joy, pure energy, pure wonder and pure amazement in a child. As adults, we forget how captivating that is. We tend to be extremely professional and we never raise our voice above a certain decibel and, of course, we can't sound excited because that just wouldn't be 'professional'. Baloney. People who are excited excite people! Emotion is energy in motion. As one of my mentors, T. Harv Eker, says, 'everything is energy'. So if you know that, use it to your advantage! If I'm excited about something and I can't wait to tell you about it, it's going to be very hard for you to ignore me.

WRIGHT

So, how do you know if you're communicating poorly?

WILSON

Are people looking away? Do they have that glazed look in their eyes? If you're speaking to an audience, are they fidgeting in their seats? You see, we forget how to read signs. If you're not connecting with someone, you know it. Have you ever been in a conversation with someone and they're looking away or they're looking behind you, or they're checking their watch, or they're doing any number of things that let you know, 'I'd rather be anywhere except here'? On the flip side, have you been in conversation with someone who's leaning toward you, looking into your eyes, nodding when you nod and being excited when you're excited? They are 'mirroring' what you are doing, which tells you that they're right there with you. The easiest way to tell if someone is paying attention is to do something and see if they do the same thing. For example, if you laugh and they laugh, if you lean forward and they lean forward, if you smile and they smile, if you frown and they frown. We forget to pick up on those cues. If you're getting mixed signals from your audience, or from the person you're talking to, your communication is missing the mark in a big way. It's like talking to a bored teenager. There is no doubt that they are tuning you out. If you ever want to practice, find a teenager and try to tell him or her something they need to know. That's the best way to make sure that you are either on point or you're missing the mark.

WRIGHT

So, what if I'm at a conference or in a room where other people are there doing exactly what I do, how do I set myself apart from these people?

WILSON

Let's say you're at a conference and everyone there is a financial planner, or everyone there is an attorney. There is something that YOU do that is unique. There is a way that YOU do it that's unique. There is something that your clients or customers have told you that you've helped them with, that no one else has ever been able to help them with before. So, when you're looking for that point of difference, think back to what your clients or your customers say about you. What do they praise about you? What do they say you've done for them that no one else has? Then ask them for 'results based' testimonials, not just, 'Oh, she's really great' or "I really enjoyed working with him". What specifically was it about you and what you did that made the difference? What results did you get them?

WRIGHT

So, after you've gotten your elevator speech together, what's next?

WILSON

Oh, that's when the fun starts! After you've gotten them interested, you have to keep them there. That means you have to know how to talk to people in a way that addresses their specific issues. Those are the things that I work with my clients on: How do I keep someone engaged after I've gotten their attention with my elevator speech? The elevator speech merely opens the door to the conversation. Most people make the mistake of making the elevator speech the sales pitch. It's not. It's simply the beginning of the conversation. From that point, you have to know how to ask questions in a way that people feel you're not trying to 'sell' them. We all like to buy, but we don't like to be 'sold'. There are techniques and ways to talk to people to get information and to actively listen, so that people will tell you exactly what you need to say to get them to become a client or to do what you ask. Listen in a way that makes sure that the client closes you, rather than you closing the client.

The elevator speech simply starts the conversation. Then it's about getting from 'hello' to signing on the dotted line. Very often, that's not going to happen in a first encounter. You have to network, you have to cultivate those relationships and you have to stay in touch. You have to drop in on your clients every now and then when you don't want anything, just to let them know you're thinking about them. For instance, I made one of the biggest business deals of my career because I talked to a man on a plane. I was on a flight, in coach, not first class, and I had the aisle seat. This gentleman was in the middle seat and it was obvious he didn't want to be there. It was late and I was tired, but I decided to make the best of it. I asked him about something that he was reading and we began this great conversation. And, you know how we do on planes: we tell our life story and then get to baggage claim and it's like we never met. I find that fascinating by the way. But, long story short, he mentioned something to me and it reminded me of a book that I had just purchased. We exchanged business cards and I sent him a copy of the book. He ended up hiring me. So, it's about paying attention. I'd given my elevator speech, he'd given his, we'd engaged in conversation. The important thing is that I listened to what was important to him and I followed up in a way that he absolutely was not expecting.

WRIGHT

Well that's fascinating, I really appreciate you taking all this time to answer these questions. I've heard the term elevator--as a matter of fact, someone, I was in conference with this past weekend and someone used the term elevator speech, of course you know what it is, but you don't know what it is. So I am so glad that now I know how to do it.

WILSON

Well, I hope I cleared up some of the mystery.

WRIGHT

And I think our readers are really going to enjoy this chapter, whether they're in business or not.

WILSON

Well, you know that your elevator speech is important even if you don't run a business or have a career outside of your home. You still meet people. There's still something fascinating, wonderful and special about you. You owe it to people to let them know what that is!

WRIGHT

Well, I really appreciate you taking all this time answering these questions for me today Annetta, I have really learned a lot and I am sure that our readers will.

WILSON

Thank you David, it's been a pleasure.

WRIGHT

Today we've been talking to Annetta Wilson, she is a Certified Professional Behavioral Analyst and Certified Trainer, and as we have found out here today, she specializes in presentation and communication skills coaching, and media training. Annetta thank you so much for being with us today on Coaching for Success.

WILSON

Thank you, David.

About the Author

ANNETTA WILSON IS PRESIDENT of Annetta Wilson Media Training & Success Coaching. She is a Certified Professional Behavioral Analyst and a Certified Trainer. Annetta is a business strategist specializing media training, presentation and communication skills coaching. Ms. Wilson is a talent coach for on-air journalists at CNN and is a Premier Coach for eWomen Network, the largest online networking community for businesswomen in North America. She has coached for Walt Disney World's Ambassador Program. An award-winning journalist, she worked in the broadcast industry as a news anchor, reporter, producer, talk show host and writer. Annetta was national emcee for Office Depot's Success Strategies Conference for Businesswomen in six U.S. cities. She is a member of the International Association of Coaching. She writes a monthly free newsletter, 'For Success', available at her Web site: YourCoachForSuccess.com

ANNETTA WILSON

7025 CR 46A Suite 1071 #344
Lake Mary, FL 32746
(407) 333-4744
info@YourCoachForSuccess.com
www.YourCoachForSuccess.com

Chapter 2

David Rock

DAVID WRIGHT (WRIGHT)

Today we're talking to David Rock. David is known as the Founder of the Brain-Based Approach to Coaching. As CEO of Results Coaching Systems, over ten thousand professionals have learned how to be better coaches using his models. David helps global organizations including Eriksson, HSBC, and EDS build coaching cultures. He is the author of three books including *Quiet Leadership,* published in 2006, and *Coaching with the Brain in Mind,* published in 2008. He is on the faculty at CIMBA, an international business school in Europe, and a guest lecturer at Oxford University, as well as Founder of the Neuro Leadership Summit and Institute. He sits on the board of a start-up school in New York City. David is currently completing a doctorate in the neuroscience of Leadership.

David, welcome to *Coaching for Success.*

DAVID ROCK (ROCK)

Thank you very much—thanks for having me.

WRIGHT

So, how did you develop as a coach?

ROCK

I started coaching formally twelve years ago. It came out of being involved in business myself and seeing how useful it was to have a sounding board. At the time, I was in business and really craving a sounding board that I could speak to usefully. I chose to do a long sabbatical and was thinking about what I wanted to do next. I realized that I wanted to create a way of providing that to others. I spent about two years I the mid nineties thinking about the most effective way of providing coaching, originally to business owners, and thinking about the most effective way of coaching people.

I gathered a small group of people together and we studied the whole art of being a sounding board. Over a couple of years, we developed some deep thinking. It was actually my full-time job for about a year to just sit down and take apart the whole process of coaching. Over that time, I developed a whole lot of best practice insights. I worked out the most efficient ways to coach—methods that I still use today. I'm a very hands-on person and I like to learn things by taking them apart, which is what I did back then.

WRIGHT

So what is your style of coaching?

ROCK

In the last five years I've been really focused on the brain-based approach. I very much come from what's going on in someone else's brain. Before that, I liked to cut to the chase with people. I get very impatient when people aren't being direct and actually saying what's really on their mind (it's very clear to me when people are doing that). I like to cut to the chase and I like to help people cut to the chase themselves. I guess you could call my style impatience. I've harnessed my impatience into an ability to help people get on with things instead of talking themselves around in circles.

WRIGHT

Seems as if that would save them money too because they'd be wasting time lying to you in getting to the truth, I would think.

ROCK

Well, people spend years, and years saying the same things to themselves repeatedly that they know don't make sense. I now understand why this happens. They've hit an impasse in their brain and they need someone to help them to see things from a different perspective. It's like trying to solve the same puzzle the same three ways—you can't see any other ways. It's actually a physical roadblock you hit in the brain. So yes, people spend years focusing on the same problem, the same way. What I think coaching does is help people break out of that roadblock.

WRIGHT

So how do you think you help people as a coach?

ROCK

When I coach, I help people see their own thinking. This is an important point and it relates to the style question as well. There are some coaches who still give lots of advice and suggestions about what you should do differently. There are many coaches who will want you to talk all about your feelings and really get into your emotions. I don't fit into either of those models. It's not that I avoid feelings and emotions—I'm quite comfortable with them. What I do is I help people see their own thinking so that they can see where their thinking is basically gone astray.

The people I coach think, "Wow, that's a crazy way of thinking that I have there; I've got to think of a different one." And that's actually where I've found that that's actually the fastest way to coach—you don't get any resistance that way. Whereas, if you're giving advice or getting into the feelings, you tend to get caught in these conversations that involve people fending you off. So what I do is I simply help people notice their own thinking and correct them. Not that their thinking is wrong or right or anything, I just help them see it notice the patterns in it. And they get it. People are very smart, the brain is incredible.

If I talk to someone a few minutes about his or her career, I might repeat what I've heard the person say. The way I do it is specific. I might say, "You've just told me that you've been thinking about a new job every day for four years. The total hours that you've spent thinking about that is probably seven hundred and so far, aside from thinking about it for seven hundred hours, you've not actually done one specific thing. I don't want to make that right or wrong, but how does that make you feel to notice that?"

The stark reality of people's thinking is quite interesting, often they have insights and something changes. My approach is to be very respectful and help people see their own thinking so they can correct it without my having to intervene too much.

WRIGHT

So what got you interested in the brain as a coach?

ROCK

I wanted to understand how it all works. I've just described my approach and I described other approaches—giving advice and focusing on feeling. I wanted to understand how those two approaches and all the other approaches worked, why they worked, and why they didn't work. By then I had spent about six years doing coaching, teaching coaching, training, and worked with thousands of coaches. By seven years into my business, I had trained three or four thousand coaches in ten countries. I really wanted to understand why it was all working because that was important to me.

To make a long story short, I was working at NYU, helping them build a coaching certificate program, and I built a theory course for them. While I was teaching this theory of coaching course, it became clear that the theories of coaching that were out there were very complicated or there were too many of them. Nothing was really clear. It happened by accident that I started to include things about brain research, which began to make so much more sense. It was a lucky accident in a sense. I was teaching classes and teaching twelve different approaches—twelve different sets of theories—and every time we taught the brain theory, everyone understood it so much better; it made so much more sense. It made students appreciate and understand coaching better too.

WRIGHT

So what do you think knowing about the brain is helpful to coaches?

ROCK

Yes, it's helpful on several levels. The first one is that it creates better coaches. People coach better when they understand the brain—it's that simple and that's an important fact. People literally coach better knowing about the brain, and they do that because they're actually really paying attention to the other person's state.

By understanding the brain, you're really interested in the brain so you're really paying attention to the other person's state of mind. Instead of getting lost in your own theories and your own strategies and concentrating on what are you going to say next, you really pay attention to the other person. You will acquire more information and make better decisions when you're doing that. You will see really important things. So the first reason is that it simply creates better coaches. They coach better in the moment if they understand what's going with other people.

The second reason is that it's so easy to train people as well. It's a little bit easier to train people who might be a little resistant to the idea. If you've got some people who normally say that they don't think that coaching is important, it's much easier to get them on board when you're introducing the brain perspective.

WRIGHT

So what are some of the surprises that you uncovered about the brain?

ROCK

There are so many. One of the most important ones is the realization that attention creates change in the brain. The brain is incredibly changeable, it's more like a forest than a computer—it's constantly changing. We actually have a big influence on each other. The questions you ask can have a big influence on someone's brain—a different word or a slightly different phrase causes people to focuses differently. At the same time, it's really hard to focus attention—people don't focus their attention very much, very often.

Another surprise is just how biological so many of the things we see in coaching are. If you understand the brain, you can really see what's going on in the biology, physically. You can understand what people are going through physically in their brain, and you get to see when people are stuck on a problem forever and you can understand how that works and why they're stuck.

Yet another surprise is in the area of feelings. It turns out that putting emotions into words—labeling your feelings—is extremely useful. But if overdone, it's not as useful. If you reactivate emotional experiences and talk about emotional events, it actually increases the emotions rather than decreasing them. Again, it comes back to where you put attention. It's useful to be able to label emotions and to be able to understand them, but only at a fairly high level—at a symbolic level. If you focus only on the emotions, they take on an energy and life of their own. It feels engaging to talk about emotions, but it doesn't necessarily create change. It's interesting, but not useful, that's the problem.

One of the other surprises about the brain is that it is wired to focus on the negative. Compare a negative and a positive word, for instance. A negative word might be "vomit," a positive word might be "love." Those two words have completely different effects. The negative word affects the brain much faster, much more deeply, and much longer than the positive word. You can sense that yourself, but it's really clear in scientific studies of the brain. Once you get one negative, the greater the chance of another thing being perceived negatively. The brain works in spirals—downward spirals or upward spirals. It's very, very interesting to see just how in tune we are to always focusing on the negative, which is another reason coaching works—coaches help people lift their thinking back up to what's possible, instead of what's not possible.

WRIGHT

How do you help organizations build coaching cultures?

ROCK

That's a great question. I work with large companies to get many people thinking about and doing coaching. In particular, I work in two areas. I help develop teams of internal coaches. Internal coaches are those a company develops from its leadership pool to be coaches for its people who have high potential. I train and certify internal coaches in a quite a large way in organizations.

I also hold a lot of programs to give leaders the skills of coaching. One is developing internal coaches to recertify. They coach for maybe an hour a week. I give them the skills to use every day. I work with large organizations to build out a program, usually across hundreds of thousands of people, to imbed the skills across the group. There's quite a lot of consulting involved, including planning and strategizing. Then we dive in and start training. There has to be a lot of coaching of people—you can only coach people to learn to coach, you can't really train them.

WRIGHT

Why are internal coaches important?

ROCK

Some companies have relied on external coaches a lot. It is considered a better idea because people think you need the confidentiality. Actually, when you really sit down and look at the differences, I'm not sure it actually makes sense for a small company (five hundred employees or fewer) to use coaches in-house. One of the reasons for the size issue is that once you get to a certain number of employees, you can coach people you've never met or who don't work with in the same group. It actually feels like they're from a different firm in many ways, and you can manage confidentiality.

WRIGHT

So is that an ongoing process?

ROCK

I recommend internal coaches where the coach might work with someone for three or up to six months and then they'll take on a different group of people. These coaches become usually high potential coaches and coaches for the people who have a great career ahead. These coaches work for maybe three or six months with a different person each time. The coaches are usually leaders—people who are busy and coach maybe one or, at the most, two people at a time. I find it a tremendous benefit to use senior leaders to be coaches rather than external ones. It's not just the fact that it's 10 percent of the cost, it's also the benefit the leaders get and the unity that's created across the group—the relationships and the learning that stays in-house. Also, when you do this you tend to actually retain employees, whereas when you use external coaches you tend to lose more people.

These people sometimes get stuck on the confidentiality issue, which is actually the smaller issue. Again, it comes back to the nature of the brain latching on to fears easily. People latch onto the fear that they have to be external without really thinking it through and looking for ways to management that. There are much bigger challenges than that for external coaches. With external coaches, the information leaves the organization, a network is not created to increase the likelihood of people leaving, you're paying extraordinary amounts of money, and it's relatively hard to manage and find the right cultural fit. There are also other disadvantages, but people never think about them because they just get stuck on the first issue.

WRIGHT

When I think of coaching, sometimes think of athletics. Coaches of athletes make millions of dollars. Does the brain-based approach to coaching apply to coaches in any industry?

ROCK

Absolutely. I teach executive coaches and business coaches, but the principles are very similar to any type of coaching. If you know how to be an executive coach, you essentially know how to help someone plan better. You also know how to help people improve their goal-setting, their organization, their personal organization, be more focused, be more honest with themselves and others, and be better communicators. All of those things are extremely useful in many settings in other than in just a company setting. So there are definitely a lot of crossover skills.

For example, everyone knows that having goals work. Well, why do they work? There's a clear explanation from the brain-based perspective. It's hard to understand exactly why goals are important unless you're aware of *why* goals are important. So in all of those cases, just having that deeper understanding can be very helpful in a lot of other fields, even being a parent.

WRIGHT

So your clients learn faster. As I understand it, one of the assets that you offer your clients is non-directive therapy, right?

ROCK

I don't like the word "therapy"—I'm not a therapist. I work with people who have achieved success and I try to help them be even more successful. What I offer them is a way to improve their thinking, not because there is anything wrong with their thinking, but to improve it. So yes, my tagline for my organization is facilitating positive change by improving thinking. What I do as I help people grow and develop is to help them think better. Instead of telling them what to do, I simply help them think through what they're interested in, in a more effective way.

WRIGHT

So are you saying that if you talk about their problems, they focus on their problems?

ROCK

Usually yes.

WRIGHT

That does make sense.

ROCK

If you talk about solutions, you make connections with solutions. If you talk about problems, you make connections with problems. The question has to be, which one is more useful? Usually talking about solutions is much more useful than talking about problems.

WRIGHT

So what's the best thing about your job?

ROCK

It's probably the people I get to meet and work with and the community that I get to be a part of. I work with many positive people who are doing things with their lives, not just sitting around waiting for life to happen. I work with people who are interested in the world. I get to travel a lot and meet really smart people who are passionate about what they do.

Then for myself, more personally, it's hard to be anything but my best self because I have so many coaches around—ten thousand to be exact.

WRIGHT

That would be nice.

So what's next up for David Rock—what's next in your career?

ROCK

I'm just finishing a new book at the moment, which is based on the concept of a day in the life of the brain. It's a story of two and their day at the office—all of the challenges that they face. It explains what's going on in their brain. I think it will be a tremendously useful text to anyone working with people, and anyone working on the job. It's an exciting book.

I think what's next for me is teaching people more widely about understanding their brain.

WRIGHT

Well, what a great conversation, David. I've learned a lot here today and I know our readers will also. I really appreciate the time you've taken with me to answer all these questions. Your concept of brain-based coaching is fascinating.

ROCK

It's been my pleasure. I have enjoyed putting it together. If there is one takeaway to remember about the brain it's that where you focus your attention changes the brain. So the first step is to be aware of where you're putting your attention; that's how you change your brain.

WRIGHT

Today we've been talking with David Rock. David is founder of the Brain-Based Approach to Coaching and he is CEO of Results Coaching Systems. David helps global organizations build coaching cultures. I don't know about you, but I really enjoyed this chapter and I think he knows what he's talking about; at least I'm going to read his next book about the concept of a day in the life of a brain.

David, thank you so much for being with us today on *Coaching for Success.*

ROCK

You're very welcome.

About the Author

David Rock ais known as the Founder of the Brain-Based Approach to Coaching. As CEO of Results Coaching Systems, over ten thousand professionals have learned how to be better coaches using his models. David helps global organizations including Eriksson, HSBC, and EDS build coaching cultures. He is the author of three books including *Quiet Leadership,* published in 2006, and *Coaching with the Brain in Mind*, published in 2008. He is on the faculty at CIMBA, an international business school in Europe, and a guest lecturer at Oxford University, as well as Founder of the Neuro Leadership Summit and Institute. He sits on the board of a start-up school in New York City. David is currently completing a doctorate in the neuroscience of Leadership.

DAVID ROCK

davidrock@workplacecoaching.com
www.DavidRock.net
www.QuietLeadership.com

Chapter 3

Dr. Pam Brill

THE INTERVIEW

DAVID WRIGHT (WRIGHT)

Today we're talking to Dr. Pam Brill. Dr. Brill understands the challenges of changing behaviors to turn visions into strategic actions that get results. Her respected authority on the dynamics of performance at the individual and team level as leadership coach, team development coach, organizational consultant, and strategic change facilitator, Pam consults with individuals, teams and entire organizations across functions including senior leaders, manufacturing floor production workers, mid level management, and C level leaders of the Fortune 500 and Fortune 20 as well as sports teams, athletes, and their coaches.

A licensed doctoral psychologist, Pam completed her pre-doctoral internship in clinical psychology at Dartmouth Medical School where she later served as adjunct assistant professor of psychiatry, coaching psychiatrist and psychologists in training. She has consulted with coach executives, leaders, and team members from a variety of industries including State Street Bank, the Offices of the United States Senate, BAE Systems, and most of the major defense contractors; Ernst and Young, Northwestern Mutual Life, Dartmouth College, Harvard University, law firms, medical centers, sales professionals in the retail and financial services industries, elite athletes, collegiate and professional athletic coaches, artisans, sales team members at Simon, Pierce, Glass, and a former GE engineer turned professional race car driver. So having said all of this, Pam welcome to *Coaching for Success.*

PAM BRILL (BRILL)

Thank you for having me and I'm honored to be interviewed by you.

WRIGHT

Well the focus of your work has been on teaching clients to implement sustainable strategic changes in order to reach higher levels of achievement, particularly peak performance under high pressure. I know that you use a term from sports, the peak performance state that athletes refer to as being in the zone, you even say that the zone applies to everything that we do and that we can achieve our highest levels of achievement and satisfaction by learning to purposefully get into this physical and mental state, whether it's to reach for work or life goals to face down the ferocious competitors in the business or a life altering illness, or even relax with your family, your dog, or the remote and the television.

What is the zone, can you describe that state, the zone for peak performance and how it relates to other areas of life. You say to every area of life, could you tell us about that?

BRILL

Absolutely, because I am passionate about this. I learned about the zone as a runner, as a college age girl, I was a working girl through college I had a lot of pressure on me, and I took to running even before those swish embossed shoes that Phil Nike came up with and it offered for me a place of complete relaxation even while my feet and legs were pounding the pavement. To put it in perspective I am around 5' 3," my inspirational height is 5' 4," and I tend to be a lean kind of person from genetic endowment. So I was really good at running, and I found this kind of odd state where I was working really hard, and yet I was totally relaxed and centered. Nothing, I was like Teflon, all the pressures of my life just bounced off of me for those minutes or hours that I ran.

So later, in a completely different place in life, I'd tell people that I discovered the zone, running the streets, and I figured out its value in my first working role. I started my career working street corners in courtrooms.

So not as a woman of the night, but as a social worker, a young social worker, working with juvenile offenders and with abused kids and traumatized kids, but most of my work was on the streets with the juvenile offenders and sometimes in their part time home and the jail, the youth development center they called it. But this came to be a value to me when I faced a potentially life altering experience when one of the fathers of a juvenile offender I had been working with, one of the fathers whose eyes were crazed, started flailing his arms and flashing this thing at me. The first thought that I had was, oh my gosh that's a switch blade, I saw that on West Side Story and it looks just like it in real life. Then I was jolted to the reality of this father was yelling things at me like I'm going to slash your pretty face off and I remember thinking, well I don't really think I'm that pretty, and then realizing, holy crow, I need to get engaged in this or I could lose my face or my life.

I just jolted into this state of engagement where I got my energy to the right place, I built momentum and I built a sense of meaning to what's in it for him, to not do that to me. I engaged him, I got ramped up, because he was ramped up on some kind of drug, but with reason still operating for me I created some meaning for this man to put his blade down, he didn't give it up, but to put it down and to realize that it wasn't in his best interest and that I was aligned with his goals of doing what was right for his son as well and for him to focus on what was possible if he changed his mind and his behaviors and his intent.

So that's really how I learned that power of engagement. It was before people were writing about engagement; this was in the early '80's, so that ages me, that's why my bio was so long. It was a lesson that I then took to learning how to engagement with my clients to get them to consider doing things differently. I remember I talked to one of my juvenile center clients into turning around the stolen car that he was driving, that he crossed state boarders in, and this was when you called me from me from a payphone, I talked him into turning it around. I created a vision for him of what would happen if he kept going in that direction, and what could happen for him if he turned the car around and I negotiated a deal for him with the local police, and he drove back into the state we were in knowing that blue lights would be flashing and people would be awaiting him. So it was about how do you engage people to do things that perhaps that they're not even thinking of, that are in their best interests.

Then I went on to talk a guy out of shooting me with a--the first time I saw a gun, went through the same thing, I'd seen this, is that a Clint Eastwood magnum, oh gee I better get in the zone. So for me it's about, if you think right now of a time when everything was clicking and you were so immersed in the moment to the challenge at hand, that all of the things that were irrelevant slipped away, your attention was focused on what was relevant and important, your energy, what I called activation, was aligned at just the right level, whether you were ramped up or relaxed and you had that attitude of winners, of being proactive, confident, playing to win, being focused on what you could do.

WRIGHT

So how did you conclude that state of engagement and its impact on performance and satisfaction that extended well beyond the sports?

BRILL

Well I did, I'm a self proclaimed nerd and my daughters would laugh and say, oh yea if they heard me say that. So when I realized that there is a name for this state, athletes call it the zone, and remember I grew up watching sports with my dad, initially gathered around a small TV an sometimes my favorite thing was when he would take me to a Bruins, or Celts or a Red Sox game. So I hope I don't alienate people with that Red Sox thing by the way, but I realized on that street corner that the same thing that athletes, that state of engagement that they went into when they did their best was where I had been. I started to read original research from the world of Sports Science, which was in it's infancy at that point by the way, and then from the World of Flow, a concept that Dr. Mihaly Csikszentmihalyi developed. He initially called this state the Optimal Performance State, an optimal experience, but his research wasn't with athletes, it was with people who had disabilities, with people who had to face life altering shifts, going from walking with their legs one day to being in wheelchairs the next.

So I took his work that showed that people can engage with any challenge and with any circumstance if they can develop a sense of meaning with what they're doing and if they can develop that momentum, and if they can focus on that half full. So I took that from research and then I looked at the people that I worked with. I moved from working with abused kids and juvenile offenders to lighten it up, and worked in a medical clinic, a

Dartmouth affiliated medical clinic, with people like you and me who were facing life altering and sometimes life threatening injuries and illnesses, as well as challenges of work. So that was where I started to engage them with the as-is of what they faced.

WRIGHT

Engaging others, I see how that is critical to pitching a baseball and/or a new idea or sales pitch.

How does this idea of engaging others relate to leadership, to effectively leading?

BRILL

Well I'm sure that you are familiar with a lot of the research by Gallup, Powers, and Perrin, and other consulting groups that got on this bandwagon of the value of the soft stuff including engagement. So they have articulated the ROI, the value that when people are engaged with their work they're more productive, they generate profit, they stay around longer, retention rates are higher. So a lot of the important factors to successful business have been associated with engagement and that was after I was working with my clients on engaging whether I was taking them down a ski hill for a retreat, an active retreat albeit, or working with them on how are we going to engage people to turn this strategy into action.

So it terms of leading I came to conclude early on, from my work with elite level athletes, and then with business people that the best contributors, whether they were called leaders or not, you had to engage people with the work at hand with what I call the as-is; this is what we've been given, this is the as-is, we could wish about the if-only, that will get us nowhere. Let's look at what our challenge is, what our obstacles are and let's engage with it and engage others that we need, that we want, to get this done. So for me I started talking about the concept of leading is engaging. It's engaging people with challenge and with change and I know you won't be surprised by this figure, it's pretty appalling, whether we're talking about people making changes to promote health, or people turning high level loss to business strategy into action to achieve that, it's a meager 25 to 30% of changes that are successfully implemented. So I started teaching and coaching my clients whether they were the leader or the team member, about how to override resistance to change and how to engage with it and succeed.

WRIGHT

Your own career has traversed many areas or arenas as a doctoral level psychologist, could you tell our readers about that, and how you maintain this thread of teaching and coaching individuals and groups to engage in order to do and feel their best?

BRILL

Absolutely. I would say that when I look back the early work that I did even before I started using the concept of being in the zone and learning to be aware of and adjust these three elements of experience that I talk about, the three A's, even before I started using that model I learned that I got my best results, whether it was play therapy or going to court to represent a child who had been abused, and would get beat up by these lawyers who were representing the alleged abuser. I got my best results when I could stay focused and remember the mission and meaning for why I was doing some of these things that weren't so pleasant and could really maintain my energy.

I remember being in court and I was testifying on behalf of a child and these lawyers would get up and really try to intimidate me and get me out of the zone, into that other state that I call the ozone, where your heart is racing and you're fingers are clenched into fists, and you're sweating and you're focused on making mistakes and half empty and in that state you can't think clearly. Now brain science confirms that our brain starts to shut down. But I remember being in that witness stand, thinking oh my god if I look down now I'll bet that I and everyone in this courtroom can see my heart beating out of my little cable knit sweater that I'm wearing and I looked down and I could not see my heart but I realized that I need to breath, I need to use some of those strategies that I learned when I studied biofeedback as a younger intern.

So I started to breath and I realized that that opened up my focus and my thinking became more clear and I started to take the time to ask for clarity from these lawyers, and I remember that I had mastered being in the zone in that setting, when one of the lawyers started to sweat, I saw this bead of sweat run down his nose, and when he told the judge that I was being a hostile witness, I realized that wow I'm in the zone and he is not. So I took that, I really took it to the streets, I taught those same techniques to athletes, I taught those same techniques to people I was working with in medical settings who were facing down grueling chemo, this was before chemo had any user friendly element to it, and then into the world of competitive sports and business, and that's what I still teach.

WRIGHT

You teach clients the value of engaging, living in the zone as you say, its life altering in that it impacts many aspects of our lives, can you tell us what is in it for anyone to pursue this state of peak performance and engagement, and what is the value of engaging besides peak performance?

BRILL

You know that' probably the shortest answer thus far. The value is a sense of pride in being involved, in being invested, in getting things done and addressing your life and challenges and teaching other people how to do that. The value is a sense of satisfaction, that pride of doing your best, of living on purpose and with passion.

WRIGHT

In your book, The Winner's Way, you go well beyond describing the zone, you teach readers how to identify when they are in the zone, and when they're not. And I think you called it a few minutes ago, the other state is ozone, then you describe a system that anyone can use, a straightforward way to systematically get into or back to the zone, engaged with the challenge at hand; giving their all and doing their best. You say it's as simple as the three A's of the winners way. What are those three A's?

BRILL

Well this is what is making me smile. These three A's, as I call them are real first of all. The first is activation, that's that sense of physical energy, it's physical and physiological, it's your beating heart, it's your sweat glands, it's the tension in your head, or the lack thereof, it's the tension in your lower back, it's the sense that butterflies may have inhabited your gut. So activation is the first one. I'll let you know as an aside that in the science literature, Behavioral Medicine and Psychology, activation is called arousal, the arousal of your nervous system. But the first team that I taught this to at Dartmouth College was the men's swim team.

There I was eager, with this little flip chart, I think I had stolen my kids Fisher Price flip chart board and they're sitting their on the pool deck in their Speedos, so I'm facing 20 athletes in Speedos and I wanted to teach them about the three A's, and I realized oh I'm not going to say arousal in front of these boys. So I circled to the other two and circled back and by then I had recouped and I was in the zone, I call the activation. But it's activation/arousal and oh by the way, they were also nerds like myself, most of them had read most of the research and some things I had written in the second year when I called the activation the older guy started laughing and told the freshmen that it was really arousal.

So the first one is activation/arousal, the second is attention, that's our focus. Attention is always selective, that's what sometimes drives us to call other people difficult because they're selecting a different piece of the reality that is facing us, than we might be and responding to that. So the second one is attention, and I go into a pretty fair amount of detail about that and teach people how attention is selective, not just by choice, but it may be that just as our fists looks different, our brains look different and that determines whether that we gravitate naturally to the big picture, or the bottom line bullets or the excel spreadsheet details or the people and process.

So we've got activation/arousal, attention, and then the third I call attitude, I wanted to make it simple for athletes and clients, but attitude isn't' looking in the mirror and saying, I like myself, because on even a good day that's not where I start in the morning, I'm not a morning girl. Attitude is those assumptions and beliefs I bring to a challenge about myself, about others, about the challenge itself and when we are engaged our activation or energy is matched for the challenge at hand, whether it's asleep at the wheel or over the top high, and our attention is focused on the critical elements and our attitude is one of being proactive rather than reactive of playing to win, where we do our best versus playing not to lose, where we may win but we won't put out to do our best. It's an attitude of purpose and confidence.

WRIGHT

So you're saying these three A's are real and describe a systematic relationship between these three elements of experience, the three A's, and it's shaped like an upside down U. can you describe their basis in reality and that relationship and the research that supports it?

BRILL

Absolutely, absolutely, the three A's are real because they're based in our nervous system and the natural chemicals that are constantly flowing through us, through our brain and our organs, through our blood. In the parts of our brain that light up and all of these are related and in that physical tension that is our sign, the heartbeat as well, of what's going on with these three A's.

So the first being activation/arousal we're able to tune into that. The second attention, we're sometimes not as aware of our attention, and attitude is carried in our self talk. The way they're related in, in a shape that looks like an upside down U. So if you could picture a line that goes up, a vertical axis, and a line that goes across at the bottom of that, so it's like an L if you would, or the left and bottom parts of the square, and above that picture an upside down U. the way they're related is the horizontal axis, the line going across, represents each of those three A's; activation, attention, and attitude. The line going up and down, the vertical axis represents performance and engagement, and they're related one on one, as you get more engaged you're performance improves.

So as we go along this upside down U, we go up the side of the upside down U until we get to the top curve at the top, an arc, that's what I call the Arc of Engagement. So for any challenge there is an optimal upside down U and an arc, and as we go along the bottom axis, as we get more energized, as our nervous system becomes aroused, our tensions become optimal, that chemistry flowing through us is optimal, when we get to that ideal level of energy or activation, we're at the top of that curve in the arc of engagement, where we're doing out best. That's where you'll see that performance and engagement are at their peak.

When we get too activated, when our hearts starts racing too fast, when we get into that ferocious state that we sometimes call anger, when we get too ramped up with activation our performance and engagement start to plummet; what we know from brain science now is that attention is related at that optimal level of attention at the top of the arc, we're focused on those things that are important and critical. When we get too ramped up, when our nervous system gets aroused, and this is just--I mean it's amazing, but makes sense--our attention actually gets narrow. The parts of our brain that enable us to shift attention and be flexible in our attention, actually those connections start to shut down. So attention, arousal, activation are related.

The third A is also related. Attitude, our ability to entertain that also is related. As we get too activated attention narrows and the parts of our brain related to attitude that enable us to entertain different ways of thinking, different points of view, to think critically, and strategically, those shut down, the front part of our brain, that beautiful last part in, in development actually starts to shut down and that's why stress and change, when we get too ramped up, really do make us stupid.

WRIGHT

So what do you mean when you say that the three A's are contagious, that our level in engagement, or disengagement, can drive other people to the same state?

BRILL

Well I'm going to explain that and then I'm going to give you examples from my own life because I can go into that ozone state as well. Have you ever been around someone who was really ramped up and people might be saying, oh that person is so uptight or they're angry or they have road rage, but soon you start to feel your own heart get that faster pace. There is research that shows that when we are with other people, whoever is dominant; their level of activation, their focus starts to be the dominant one. That can be both good and bad. In fact they've looked at a jazz group and when they initially get together their brainwaves are not on the same wavelength, and then as their brainwaves start to get into the same wavelength, their music improves, they're in the groove as they would say in music. So this is an important fact for leaders, for salespeople, for parents. You know if you want to get other people engaged with you, it's important to understand that our level of engagement can often drive people to that same level of engagement, or disengagement.

So I'll give you two examples. One is a great example, remember I was traveling with my four kids when they were younger, we were traveling back from Colorado, we got into Denver, a big snow storm had closed the airport down and so there were hundreds of people waiting to get on a flight and our flight was overbooked. So there I am with my husband, four kids, and myself, six of us and I needed to get back the next day, I had some big consulting gig or something I needed to get home, pack and get out. So the people in front of us were yelling and screaming at this poor airline person and the person said, I'm sorry I can't get you on the flight. So they went away angry; they were activated, they were focused on negativity, their attitudes were bad. I, in the meantime, decided that the only way I'm getting anywhere is to breathe and get in the zone. So I stepped up, looked at this poor person with compassion and said rough day huh? And they looked so relieved; I could see their heartbeat go down. So I just explained, I'm a working mom, I'm weary just as you are, if you can help me, I really need your help. I explained the situation. In the meantime my husband was over across the way, he was like over activated, talking to customer service. This person, not only did the person I spoke to get us on a plane, but when I gave the tickets to my kids, one of my kids is more observant than I said, said, wow, we were like in 2A, 2B and I said oh they must start the numbers again when they get to coach. So they went over and got their dad, we get on this plane, and guess what, we were in first class, all six of us. So it's contagious.

WRIGHT

How is coaching for peak performance different from other types of coaching, and how is your Winner's Way system different from other methodologies directed at performance, say the behavioral coaching system you learned from working shoulder to shoulder as a co-coach apprentice with the highly esteemed Marshal Goldsmith, or from other sports psychology consultants too?

BRILL

Thank you, that's a great question. There is a lot of overlap because the system that I've developed, the Winner's Way is based on cognitive psychology to teach people how to change their beliefs, that's the attitude piece; it's based on mind/body medicine. Herb Benson, and the Relaxation

Response, that's the activation piece and it's based on perceptual and brain psychology as well and the power of attention and what we're learning now about how point of view maybe hardwired into our brain structure and how can you change that and then it's based on this whole other body of research that demonstrates that the mere thought of change, the just visualizing things, will set our nervous system on fire, and get our muscles twitching as if we were really doing that.

So I do focus on behavior, as does Marshal Goldsmith and I also focus on the power of belief, changing one's beliefs that could bring you to a situation where your mind is closed and your heart is closed and you can't get engaged. And I very, very much focus working with people on what is the challenge that you're going to face, what's the ideal level, what does that ideal upside down U look like, where do you want your level of activation be, what do you want to be focused on, what are the attitudes and beliefs that you want to bring, what kinds of language do you want to use?

So I teach them to identify the optimal place they want to be and then I teach them how to identify the markers that suggest that they're either their nervous system is getting under activated, their focus is getting too broad, or they're starting to become laissez-faire in attitude or the other side where they're starting to get ramped up too tight to be engaged, and their attention is narrowing and their attitude is becoming one of ferocious, play not to lose, and they've lost sight of what we're really doing here. So I teach people to put words and sensations to what it means to be in the zone, and the ozone, and then I work with a technique that started out in mind/body medicine with cancer patients, teaching them how to visualize the cancer cells being eaten up by radiation or by chemotherapy, and that kept them in a relaxed state that was associated with better healing and better treatment.

I teach in sports that same relaxation and visualization has been proven to be related to performance improvement. So I take it to the real world, I have my clients learn to get relaxed themselves using a strategy, a technique I use, a variation of progressive relaxation and I teach them how to visualize the challenge that they'll face, or one that they faced where they didn't like the outcome and they get themselves into that state of the zone. Then believe it or not I teach them how to move into the ozone where they're disengaged and they're feeling discombobulated and how to get themselves back in, so by the time they've gotten there they're nervous system has already been there, it feels like they've already been there and done that, they have a sense of mastery, especially over situations that they didn't do so well, whether it's a pitch, an all hands meeting that you're leading, or getting bad new, whatever it may be, they feel like they've been there, they've done it, they've mastered that and they feel equipped that should they start to lose that edge they know how to get back. And that's really what great athletes like tiger woods and others do. It's not that they're always in the zone, it's that they know how to get back, and that to me is also what is resilience and what is that trait that we all need now more than ever in this flattened world, and stressful economy.

WRIGHT

So what drives people out of the zone, how can we identify the things that get to us that keep us from stepping up or even from dreaming and doing something fulfilling or making meaning out of the ordinary and appreciating the moment?

BRILL

Isn't that really our goal in life, to appreciate the moment and make meaning out of the ordinary or the curve balls that are thrown to us? What drives us out and this is what I learned from decades of research, looking at what drove people to those other states of being frazzled or just in apathy, cause those are the opposites of the zone. What drives us out is a sense of perceived threat. Think about our language, and bare assed, that's being not adequately covered, a sense that I may lose something, and we see this in change, the reason we resist change and even health promoting change is that we fear being out of our comfort zone. We fear that which is uncertain, more than what we have that may be uncomfortable. So what drives us out of the zone is that sense of perceived threat, I might lose here, and it's subtle and it's not so subtle, we see it in the workplace where people throw barbed words at each other and if we look back and we can video the meeting we could see that something happened where that person felt like they're stance or their point of view is threatened and so they threw barbed words to threaten the other person and then it just kind of falls apart and people are not longer listening and they're just protecting their turf, and so that's part of it.

How can we identify the things that get us out? Well it really is, that's how I work with my clients, individuals and teams, what are the instances that got you off your game? In sports it may be easy, most athletes will always tell me there's a particular team, or particular athlete, who just the mere thought of that person gets me sweating bullets or makes me not want to get out of bed and go to the competition. In life we have similar things, people that we might face down at work, we call them difficult, and in reality, it's that they have a different point of view, and a different point of view can often be enough that we experience it as a threat, rather than understanding that in this day and age differences are no longer threatening, life threatening, they're actually key to our survival.

I'll just stray into one tangent which is that there is a line of research called, I think it's social anthropology, and some of the brain scientists have been looking at this and saying, you know the reason that the mere thought of change can get people into the ozone and over activated and stupid in the face of change or stress is that as a species we've been programmed to look for things that are new, novel, or different and to attack them ferociously, as furrier versions of our species, that's what kept us alive. So another furry, standing upright creature, who smell different, which smelled fishy, could be there to steal your cave or kill your off spring, or you. A plant that looked different or smelled fishy could be toxic. So we still can go into that state of threat with novelty, change and different, and yet now we have this outer layers of our brain, this beautiful cortical layer that when it's working well, when you're at the top of that U and it's working well you can actually understand and entertain different points of view and realize, hey it's with these differences that we're going to survive and thrive.

WRIGHT

Can you tell me more about the role of pressure and stress, including change on driving us out of the zone?

BRILL

Absolutely. That's in all of that research that I just referenced that's been done, in one line of research, research is why are people are up in their chemistry when they just think about stress or change and the chemistry that we elicit is this full force flood that bathes our brain and nervous system, it sounds lovely the bathing part but it's actually horrific, that's where we get over activated, our focus narrows, and our attitude become what I call the language of misery, rather than the language of mastery; oh bother I have to do this, I can't do this, I need to do this, instead of when we're more centered then our chemistry is more appropriate when we go into the language of desire and mastery; so in this miserable state.

Another line of research looks at what happens to the brain when the mere thought of change or stress is introduced, and what happens is that outer cortical layer that I mentioned, the beautiful part that enables us to entertain different points of view and to think abstractly and to be compassionate shuts down and we literally become stupid. Our attention narrows, we hold tight to our narrow point of view and our assumptions and we defend those tooth and nail, with our teeth gritted and our jaws tight and our backs arched and ready to pounce over a negotiation table or conference table. So we really do become stupid in the face of change and stress.

I guess that's where I see my own mission is I love nothing more teaching people to identify that state, to laugh at themselves, at ourselves, believe me I can go there in Boston traffic to laugh at yourself and say, whoa I am ramped way too tight and to simply breath in, let go of the tension in your fists that are gripping the steering wheel or your pen and to see that point of view open and to build meaning for whatever your facing down, including change.

WRIGHT

You stress the importance of acknowledging differences, specifically differences in point of view, and that a difference is merely just that, a difference and that when we're feeling stressed we get stupid in terms of not begin able to see different angles or point of view, could you tell our readers about more that?

BRILL

Absolutely. One of the three A's as I mentioned is attention. Athletes would always telling me well the coach was yelling at me, pay attention, pay attention, but I was paying attention, but just not I guess what he or she wanted me to. So we assume that if we say pay attention, everybody is going to look at or hear the same or sense the same things, and that is--an assumption is going to get your in trouble, in general I discourage assumptive behaviors. But again I can go there my self.

So attention is one of the three A's and my approach to attention is based on the work of one of the original psychologist who got into sports science, a guy named Bob Nideffer, and Bob Nideffer conceptualized attention along two dimensions, either it's internal or external, narrow or broad. So he had four quadrants of attention and then realized that each of us has an attention style related to what we see, what we hear and how we approach problems and solutions. Now as it turns out, Bobs early work is very aligned with what other people have put forward as behavioral styles, or social styles, there's the DISC, Tony Alessandra's work, it's aligned but Bob's work is a little bit more technical which of course appeals to the nerd in social scientist in me.

So he's got these four quadrants of attention there's external narrow, those are the people who see the world in terms of bullets; tell it to me, give me the results, those would be the directive type of people. There is external broad, which are the more visionary, strategist big picture people where if they needed to remember the details they would die. There is the internal broad; those are more the people process people who before the starting line will say, is everybody really ready for this change? And then there are the internal narrowly focused people, and those are the people who see the world in excel spreadsheets for them details are what drive and could drive others crazy.

So we each have a characteristic point of view and in the face of that stress chemistry, that flood that I described, we each go to our corners and see the world problems, solutions and each other through that very narrow lens. And that's when we call each other difficult and stupid and we defend our own point of view tooth and nail and we lose sight of the common purpose or intent that may have brought us to this team or to a negotiation table. So I teach my clients how to identify their own point of view, how to identify the characteristic style or point of view of others, and I teach them how to frame issues, especially change in a way that will appeal to all four points of view and how to frame it if they're in a one on one with someone else in a way that that person will hear the what's in it for me, and build meaning for changing their point of view, for changing their behaviors and for getting on board with driving change and strategy.

WRIGHT

So could you tell our readers about a sports success story? I mean when you taught an athlete, or a team to get into the zone. How did you work with them and what were the observable results?

BRILL

Well I would like to tell you about one of my favorite clients, without using his real name, though he's given me permission to use his story. His story still inspires me. This was a high school age young man who was attending one of the elite Vermont ski academies, he was being groomed to be an Olympian, was probably about 9 months to a year away from competing at the Olympic level, he competed at the Olympic level for his age. His ski coaches called me and said, look this kid is our best skier but when it comes time to compete something happens and his performance falls apart. He can ski in the zone the day before in training and blow people out of the water for times and his courage and go-for it ability, and then in competing something happens.

So this kid, either parent would drive him like an hour and a quarter to my office, and we started working with these three A's and he got it, I knew he was getting it because he brought me an article from a ski magazine that was around similar concepts, this is really easier for me Pam I can get it three A's. So he was able to identify what it was like for the different types of races that he did, the slalom where the gates are close together and you sum them up precise in your turns, and then the other slalom race the faster slalom race where you are going at high speeds and the gates are placed far apart and you are just soaring at the speed you go in a car. So he learned to identify the different upside down U's for each of those different types of races and we watched a video and that enabled him to get a sense of when he was in the zone, and not in the zone and he started to really get-- especially with the grip on his ski poles, and the grip of his toes, and the angle of his back. He could just identify fine nuances that let him know early on that he was starting to lose it.

So he learned to use activation to get back in the zone and attention; if he was working through the gates, between the gates, at where he wanted to go, rather than at the gate, if he looked at the gate he almost skied into it. So attention was right on, if you looked at the start his focus was on what he could do and then his attitude was one of I want to do this, I love skiing, I am the most capable guy here. He was great.

So the next season his dad calls me from out of state, leaves me some times in each race they're getting better and better. Then his dad calls and it's a different tone, and his dad tells me something horrible has happened. This kid was skiing in the fast race, snowmobile crossed into the race course, totally illegal, driven by a couple of teenagers, and he hit is flat on, he went up in the air, was in a coma of sorts, his legs had been mangled. That wasn't what I expected to hear. So I was in the zone for grieving, I mean I was bereft for sadness for the physical capabilities that I was concerned that this boy had lost and also the dreams. This was his dream; he had given up his teenagedom to pursue this.

So he came out of this coma, he called me when he was still flat in the bed, I started crying and he said, listen doc you are not going to lose it on me, you need to get in the zone because I'm using those three A's to get myself out of this bed and I'm going to learn how to walk and then I'm going to come into you and you're going to teach me how to get back on ski's. So I kind of said, oh I've got it, I've got it, I pulled myself back together, when I got off the phone I cried again. This kid learned to walk in record time, came back to the ski academy, came to see me and the first time he walked into my office he had those metal crutches appended to his arms, not ski poles, and he was pulling his legs along. I saw him, burst into tears, he alerted me again, get your poop and your three A's together because you're going to help me. Then he proceeded to take his shoes, his boots off to show me his mangled legs at which point I said, listen this is why I'm a psychologist and not an MD, put those boots back on, I'll help you, as long as you keep the boots on.

So he got back on skis David, he got back knowing that he would never ski at the pace or with the style that he had, but he was determined to get back on skis. He skied and I remember the first time after he had got on skis when he took his feet and legs out of those ski boots, they got swollen for days because of the internal damage still there. But he built meaning for staying in that industry; he became the youngest ski coach at his ski academy. I remember his father called me again, and I knew his father and his father said, we've got a problem, he's teaching these kids at the ski academy all of your stuff, he's teaching them those three A's. I said to his dad, no there is no problem there, those three A's are his; he made them his and good for him. He went on, this young man, to stay in the industry and to be a professional course setter. Imagine the courage, the attitude it takes to set race courses and watch people that you could have beat ski through those courses and still have your love for the game. That's my favorite sports success story. I could give you success stories of Olympic level people I've worked with, of teams that I've worked with, that other people might know, but that's my favorite story.

WRIGHT

Can you give me one more example for those of us who think we want to do something but can't get going? You call it moving yourself to action, or motivation. So how would you get me to go to a gym? Most of us our intentions are there, but our running shoes remain idle, under utilized and gathering dust near the treadmill, so how could you help us?

BRILL

Well let's start there and I'll give you one example from business as well. You know if you said to me, look my doctor has told me that I will get more miles and live better miles and go to the gym and what doctor doesn't tell us that. I'd say that, yea you know what everybody hears that and again, 25% of the people at best follow through. So I would work with you on those three A's. I'd start with the attitude, I'd ask you to create some meaning for me about why this was important to you and I'd ask you to create a vision; you go to the gym and you get your heart healthy and you keep your brain in motion and what's your life going to look like in 10 or 15 years? What are the things that you want to be doing, what's your vision? For most people there vision is their bicycling with their life partner, or their grandchildren. I've never had someone who said well you know I'm carting an oxygen tank around and I can't get out of my chair. So that's the vision.

Then I ask you to create m ore of a grim vision. Okay so if you keep going the way you are, realistically what's the vision going to be? Well you know I might have some mild memory problems, or Alzheimer's, my heart won't be as strong, it's going to be harder for me to get out of the chair, and if I can remember where my hiking boots are maybe I'll be able to hike briefly with my grandchildren, but not much. So we create two visions, a tale of two cities one might say. Then I ask you to build some meaning of why its important to you to look towards this other vision, and what needs to change, and what do you want to change? We work on that language of mastery versus misery.

I ask you each time that you think about, oh bother I have to go to the gym to turn that around, because that's what I work with on attitude adjustment, each time you say, I have to do this, I want you to change that to I want to do this, I want to go to the gym because I want to build my brain cells and my bones and be in it for the long run to go bicycling with my grandchildren. That's my vision. Then I ask you to set time aside to focus your attention to make it a priority, it might be 7 minutes initially that you're going to go to the gym, it might be longer, it might be initially that you're only going to walk to your mailbox and back 5 times a day. But we set reach goals, and we celebrate achieving each one and sooner or later you start to have an internal motivation and s sense of pride from this and it's become a habit. So using those three A's and moving yourself to action.

In the busies setting I've worked with sales people who have lost their mojo and I do the same thing, create the two visions, the tale of two cities, get you focused on the positive one, and then how are we going to adjust those 3 A's to keep you going, and to adjust your language so that you're really in that sense of opportunity versus oppression of mastery over misery.

WRIGHT

During this conversation, you have mentioned many other researchers and practitioners in this field, what makes your perspective, your point of view and your coaching model unique?

BRILL

Well thank you for asking that, I mean my work is derived from hardcore science, it is research based. The work of the early mind/body researchers Herb Benson, Carl Thorse, and the type A guy, the work of Mihaly Csikszentmihalyi on flow, the work of Marshal Goldsmith on behavioral coaching, the cognitive psychologist, it's based on all of that and between you and me I have been fortunate that I grew up with a lot of that science, that sports science guys, I presented my own original research with people who's work I had been reading and whom I was in awe, and they became my friends and mentors. So I know most of these people, I met them. I took their body of knowledge and put it together in a simple systems model that explains that why when I get ramped up, I can't find my keys and I believe that I'm not going to be on time, and that applies to everything we do. It's simple, it's easy to remember and still it works and it applies to everything we do and I have had people tell me that when they start thinking in terms of these three A's, their work results improve their sports results improve, and their relationships at home improve as well, and so does their health. So it's not that my method is so different, it that it's distilled, and it's been tested, field tested in so many experiences from the mundane, how do you maneuver traffic and end up at your office in a good mood and in the zone, to the extreme from how do you move from one day thinking that you're my business coach Pam, to the next day you're coaching me on how to get the best chemotherapy and how to advocate for my health.

WRIGHT

I'd like to thank you Pam for this informative and energizing interview, I can sense that you were in a zone with me here today. Is there anything else you want our readers, as coaches or potential users of the Winner's Way to know?

BRILL

Well I think I told you when I told you when we were talking one time earlier that I learned a lot of my life lessons from my parents. They were hard working people, they each grew up in tenements, and my dad especially orphaned at age 4, rescued by his oldest brother, his oldest brother got married and he and his wife took my dad out of a pretty harsh foster home, it would have been an Amber alert today. But my dad having been orphaned, he was a Flying Tiger in World War II, he played sports his whole life, he was recruited to play pro baseball twice, and his brother told him there was no money in that. We laugh to this day. By the way my dad when he died in my arms, we were watching a Red Sox game still, but he taught me this passion for life that you accept the as-is and you deal with that and you create visions of what could be better, not if-only, or I used to be, but how do you want to be. He taught me that life is a one shot deal; you get one journey around this globe. Lucky for me he lived to be almost 85, but he taught me to go for it, that to live life with a sense of engagement, to live it in the zone and I really believe that life is too short to live it anywhere else.

WRIGHT

Today we've been talking to Dr. Pam Brill; a respected authority on the dynamics of peak performance at the individual and team levels. A licensed doctoral psychologist, Pam has consulted or coached executives, leaders, and team members from a variety of industries. I think that we have found out here today she knows a whole lot about what she's talking about. I'm going to listen and I'm going to do, I hope the readers do the same. Pam thank you so much for being with us today on Coaching for Success.

BRILL

David thank you and my heart is beating and I am smiling as is my spirit. This has been a great experience, and you are a master at being in the zone in your line of work, so thank you.

About the Author

Licensed Psychologist, organizational development and motivational expert, Dr. Pam Brill provides clients and seminar participants with a systematic method-- *The Winner's Way* —for getting "in the Zone" to prevail over any challenge life can toss and to enjoy the journey. As President of In The Zone, Inc. Peak Performance Consulting Group , Dr. Brill provides customized consultation, coaching, and seminars to entire organizations, teams, and individuals to enhance performance and to build leadership and contributing team membership for life. With her unique Winner's Way system, people learn to engage hearts and minds--their own and others'-- and to enlist the critical energy to turn strategic visions into strategic actions.

DR. PAM BRILL
www.inthezoneinc.com

Chapter 4

N. Elizabeth Fried

WAVE GOODBYE, SAY HELLO!™

THE INTERVIEW

DAVID WRIGHT (WRIGHT)

Today we're talking with Dr. Elizabeth Fried, author, consultant, and executive coach. She is also President of N.E. Fried and Associates, Inc. For twenty-five years her firm has served more than fifteen hundred clients worldwide. A vibrant and entertaining speaker, she addresses audiences on such topics as 360 feedback, employee engagement, and coaching. She is best known in the coaching world for her pioneering alternative coaching strategies that help executives achieve their goals quickly and effectively. Dr. Fried has published three books and more than fifty professional articles. Her work has been quoted in the *Wall Street Journal, USA Today, The New York Times, The Chicago Tribune, Washington Post, US News and World Report, MS, Business Week,* and *FORTUNE Magazine.* She has also been a featured guest on over one hundred radio and television broadcasts. TheLearningEngine.org, MyExecutiveCoach.net, and Intermediaries Speakers Bureau are divisions of her firm.

Dr. Fried, welcome to *Coaching for Success.*

Dr. Elizabeth Fried (Fried)

Thank you, I'm excited to be talking with you today.

Wright

You are known for using a unique strategy that helps executives achieve their goals more quickly. Tell me about that.

Fried

For progressive clients who are open to alternative and somewhat metaphysical thinking, I use a blended approach. I combine traditional coaching techniques with an innovative methodology that I call *Wave Goodbye, Say Hello!*™

Wright

How does blending traditional coaching with an innovative technology help speed up results?

Fried

Typically, I'll use traditional assessment tools to obtain a baseline, such as 360 feedback and behavioral styles and values inventories. I'll also gather information on personal and work-related goals and help the client prioritize them. And, I always hold my clients accountable for their promises to themselves on accomplishing these objectives through standard coaching strategies. These conventional approaches are valid and helpful in achieving the desired results. However, they take longer when used alone. I'm able to boost results when I combine them with my alternative techniques.

Blending traditional methods with innovative technology speeds up the process because this technology offers an added ingredient, which does two things. First, it helps the individual clarify goals and secondly, it actually helps remove the resistant habits that stand in the way of goal achievement. By first removing the resistance to adopting new behaviors, we clear the path for quicker integration. Thus, regression to old habits is less of an issue. Clients can then move forward and assimilate positive behaviors easier and faster.

Clients usually come to me because they need to change a behavior to achieve their goals. Kicking old habits is hard, requiring a lot of practice, reinforcement, and coaching. Thus, without constant practice, backsliding can occur more readily with traditional methods alone. I use my *Wave Goodbye* methodology to clear out subconscious barriers that impede and lengthen the coaching process. By removing these subtle obstructions up front, clients can reduce their coaching time and achieve quicker results.

WRIGHT

Why is it easier to backslide when using traditional methods alone?

FRIED

We're talking about behavioral changes. Usually, when I'm coaching executives, the focus is on improving their leadership. It's difficult to change existing behaviors; it's much easier to learn new behaviors.

For example, managers have been using their current management or leadership behaviors for years. Even though they may be using poor behaviors, they are very *good* at behaving *badly*—after all, they've been practicing for years! So, when they enroll in leadership training, they're faced with having to take an existing maladaptive skill and convert it into an adaptive one. In order to do this, the maladaptive skill, which has been with them for years and has really been wired deeply in their brain through neural networks, must be disconnected before the new skill takes root. That is the challenge and change doesn't happen overnight

With traditional coaching, the client would learn a new skill, have opportunities to practice it, receive coaching, practice, practice, practice, and obtain more reinforcement and coaching until it is ingrained. This takes a significant amount of time.

For example, let's say I teach you a new skill and tell you why it's important to change your behavior. Cognitively you know it makes sense and you get it, but are you going to do it on a regular basis, or fall back on old habitual behaviors because they're easy and comfortable? Let's look at a very concrete example to demonstrate how this works.

If I said to you, "Would you like me to show you a new way to tie your shoes so they won't come untied? And the neat thing is that you don't have to double-knot them anymore and deal with the hassle double-knotting gives you when you have to untie them."

You say to me, "Yes, Elizabeth, that sounds great. Show me."

I show it to you, you're thrilled about it, and you're so excited that you even go home and you show your significant other. Both of you think it's pretty cool. That evening you go to bed, but in the middle of the night your smoke alarm goes off. You're scrambling to get your shoes on ... but ... which way are you going to tie your shoes? More than likely, you'll tie them the old way. That's because changing a skill so that it's comfortable and natural requires practice, reinforcement, practice, coaching, and more practice. And often times you get worse before you get better because you are learning and it's awkward. Tying your shoes is not a new skill. So, until you disconnect the old behavior from your brain, and replace it with a skill that feels comfortable and natural, you will fall back on your old patterns when under stress.

The same concept applies to management behaviors; however, I can shortcut that process by getting change to happen more quickly with my *Wave Goodbye* approach. This method dismantles some of those deeply embedded neural networks associated with old behaviors, allowing the individual to reduce the amount of practice and coaching needed to ingrain new behaviors.

WRIGHT

What comes to mind as an example is Tiger Woods. He is arguably the best golfer who has ever lived. But, two or three years ago he stopped what he was doing in the middle of all his wins and changed his swing; he then started to lose. Everyone thought he was nuts! He had to disconnect everything, which took quite a while, but through constant practice and coaching he is now winning like crazy again.

FRIED

He just won the 2008 U.S. Open here in San Diego. You're absolutely correct. That is a perfect example. If I could have used my *Wave Goodbye* approach on him, he might have resumed his winning streak more quickly. (I'll share a client golfing story with you later.)

WRIGHT

How do you blend the techniques? Which do you use first, and what is the actual process you go through to make goal achievement occur more quickly?

FRIED

As I mentioned earlier, I will often start with a typical assessment to get a sense of style and values. Depending on the circumstances and issues, I will conduct a 360 feedback to find out how the executive is perceived by his or her full circle of influence. That may include the manager, peers, direct reports, and customers. Then we sit down and say, "Where do you want to go and what do you want to work on?" Once that is established, I begin by removing some of the old habits that might stand in the client's way even before I address moving toward his or her goals. These habits or conditionings are called Core Dynamics of Common Problems™ that have taken place from the time the individual was a small child.

I was first introduced to the core dynamics when I attended a human software engineering seminar developed by Tom Stone, president of Great Life Technologies. Tom is an expert in the application of biophysics and changing patterns of energy in the human body. I credit him for providing me with the foundational knowledge and standard protocol. Because I knew the original labels and descriptions of the core dynamics may not appeal to my business clients, I worked with him to modify their definitions and application to the corporate world.

There are twelve core dynamics that affect all of us to some extent. The process to remove them usually takes about six to eight sessions.

WRIGHT

So how do you clear these core dynamics?

FRIED

The best way to describe this is through Tom's computer analogy because core dynamics are like computer viruses—they stand in the way of performing optimally. Let's say that you get a brand new computer and you take it out of the box; you start it, and it is running wonderfully. Then, after time, it starts to slow down because you've been on the Internet and your computer has picked up viruses, adware, spyware, and so on. When this happens, David, what is the only way to get rid of a virus on your computer?

WRIGHT

I'd take it in and get it cleaned. It is then returned to me in brand new condition.

FRIED

So you either reformat the disk to delete the virus or run antivirus software to delete the virus. Formatting the disk causes you to lose your data. If you don't have a backup, and want to keep your data, you'll probably use antivirus software and delete the virus. Correct?

WRIGHT

Yes.

FRIED

If you didn't use anti-virus software to delete the problem, and I said to you, "Hey David! I want you to see how this virus is eating up your files." Would simply making you aware of it get rid of the virus?

WRIGHT

No.

FRIED

If I said, "You know, David, if you just had a little more will power and sat in front of your computer and said, 'Virus leave!'" would that get rid of it for you?

WRIGHT

Nope!

FRIED

Right! The only way to get rid of a virus is to delete it. The same is true for these twelve core dynamics. They essentially need to be deleted in order to debug our human software so we can operate more effectively.

Here's why. As healthy babies, we start out as essentially perfect, with all the right software running smoothly. And then when we go out into the world, someone might say to us, "You can't do that," and then give us one or more reasons why, such as: you're too fat, you're too short, you're too tall, you're not quick enough, you're not pretty enough, you don't deserve that. These statements cause us to start developing conditioned responses (core dynamics), creating subtle fears that limit our performance. My job is to help clients get rid of these obstacles first, so they have a clear path toward accomplishing their goals.

We'll spend the next few minutes summarizing these twelve core dynamics and how they limit optimal performance.

1. **Limiting Possibilities.** This dynamic is based on the illusion that if you experience things fully you won't be able to handle the feelings that come up and fear you'll become overwhelmed emotionally. (And really, who among us ever wants to let anyone know we feel that we are freaking out?) This illusion comes from experiences of having been overwhelmed by intense feelings when we were very young. In order to avoid this overwhelming feeling, we make the inner decision to resist feeling things fully. Physiologically, as children, we only have so much ability to handle emotional crises because the place in our brain that is designed to handle difficult situations (spindle cells) has not matured. As adults this area grows and matures, enabling us to deal with complex situations without the fear of falling apart.

   Here's another one of Tom's computer analogies: The original PCs operated on DOS. They often crashed if given complex programs. Today, we have Windows Vista, which handles hugely complex programs that DOS could never handle. The problem with humans is that many still operate emotionally on "DOS." They don't even realize they *have* an emotional "Windows Vista" operating system, capable of handling so much more. So one of the first things I do is dismantle that perception. When you are free of this obstacle, you say, "I can feel anything without fear of collapsing into being overwhelmed." In other words, "I'm cool with it, bring it on." In business, this will help us deal with complex issues without being an emotional wreck. We are able to accept assignments that are broader in scope and enjoy the responsibility and rewards that come with them.

2. **Disregarding Your Instincts.** In this case, you are ignoring your intuition. This dynamic occurs from having been punished as a child for acting on your inner knowing, or intuition. It's based on the illusion that if you act on your intuition you're going to be overwhelmed with the consequences, such as punishment or upsetting someone. Let's say you were a kid and you had an artistic creative bent. You had this intuition that you wanted to draw so you looked for an ideal blank canvas—the wall. You had a great time with your crayons and were very proud of your work. But then, in walked your parent who spied your artistic creation and starting yelling, "What are you doing?" or maybe even smacked you. Now you think, "Well, gee, if I ever do what I feel inside of myself, I am going to get punished and make someone upset." So you don't act on your intuition and ignore that little voice. The reality is, however, if you follow your instincts they rarely betray you.

Now, let me ask you this, David. Do you tend to trust your instincts?

WRIGHT

Yes.

FRIED

What happens? Have they ever failed you?

WRIGHT

Yes.

FRIED

They failed you?

WRIGHT

Yes. Sometimes.

FRIED

Sometimes. Hmm . . . Were you truly listening to your instincts or were you applying logic? Or perhaps there was some other personal agenda operating that drowned that little voice.

WRIGHT

I have misjudged people a lot down through the years.

FRIED

That's interesting because generally, when we trust our instincts, there is a little voice within telling us whether or not we should do something. If we ignore that voice and apply logic or get distracted by a personal agenda, we are usually wrong. Generally, when we trust our instincts, we are right. Now, it could be that there was something in your particular case where you were applying thinking (instead of knowing) or personal desire. If you think back you will probably realize that on some level, you really knew what you should have done, but you quieted that voice and acted otherwise. When this happens, sometimes I will ask clients, "What were you pretending not to know?"

WRIGHT

You are probably right. I have this bad habit—character flaw actually—that wants to save everybody in the whole world. Sometimes people don't want to be saved. I always go into a relationship—business, employment, or whatever—hoping for the best. Sometimes I have been discouraged about the results.

FRIED

So, you did know it, you were just hoping that in your desire to save them, you could. But your intuition told you there was an issue. You didn't listen and you went down the rescue path. (For the record, David, you can't save people. They have to want to save themselves. For that reason, I refuse coaching clients who aren't committed to the process.)

WRIGHT

I wish you had told me that a few years ago!

Fried

It's never too late to learn—if you really want to! Basically, when we have removed the issues surrounding what keeps people from trusting their intuition, they feel that they can completely trust their intuition and always act on it. From a business perspective, trusting our instincts helps us make better choices and keeps us from going into analysis paralysis.

3. **Being Judgmental.** When we judge something or someone, we're distancing ourselves by attempting to create a feeling of being separate from it. We might say, "Hey, I'm not like that." However, in reality, the things we judge often reflect a part of ourselves that for some reason we don't want to acknowledge. We find, for example, that when we don't have any kind of charge about something, we feel neutral toward it, so we're not judging it. But, if something is causing us to feel uncomfortable, we have a habit of avoiding issues that we really probably need to address or resolve within ourselves.

   Interestingly, when this is present, we are often hardest on ourselves. We don't try things because we don't want others to judge us as we would judge others. This can paralyze us from moving forward because we want to be perfect. When we don't have this issue, we feel that everything we experience is a part of us and we acknowledge and embrace it. In business, this gives us the courage to depart from convention, try new things, and fearlessly move forward.

4. **Getting Distracted.** When this dynamic is operating, we're avoiding the present. We don't deal with the here and now and instead get lost in stories that we created about past events or we start possibly projecting negative outcomes into the future. We avoid being present because we fear that if we do stay present we won't be able to deal with whatever feelings come up.

   Remarkably, the *fear* of the feeling is often worse than dealing with the feeling itself. Many addictions that people experience are a result of a number of unresolved emotions about the past. They feel it's too intense to deal with the present. They often numb themselves with addictions whether it is smoking, eating, drinking, or drugs because they do not want to feel the intensity of what might come up if they allowed themselves to stay present.

In business, managers sometimes ignore harsh realities and bury their head in the sand because it could be too frightening to think about the business going under, job loss, or other consequences. Once this dynamic is dismantled, people feel they can live completely present and in the moment. Decisions improve.

5. **Lacking Self-Esteem.** When this dynamic is operating, we try to get a sense of ourselves from outside sources. For instance, we might define ourselves by our actions, our accomplishments, or maybe our possessions. It's based on the illusion that we are incomplete and something outside of ourselves will complete us and make us whole and contribute to our happiness. Basically we are saying, once we have that promotion, that corner office, that bonus, things will be perfect. Or, if only this person (my spouse, my boss, my parent) acted better I would be happy. Those things are outside of you, as opposed to saying, "Look. I am whole and complete as I am. And I am just fine." When this dynamic is no longer present, you have self-appreciation and are naturally happy. You recognize that external conditions do not dictate your self-worth. You are in control of your personal happiness.

6. **Seeking Validation.** Now, when this dynamic is operating, we confuse love, which is unconditional and requires nothing in return, with the need to receive something from someone else. Think of it this way: love lets go and need holds on. This dynamic is based on the illusion that love is something you get from outside of yourself. This is constantly modeled to us through our cultural conditioning, movies, songs, and media, particularly country-western songs. Our whole society talks about getting love from someone else as opposed to understanding that you need to love yourself first. So when this dynamic is no longer present, you say, "I love unconditionally and participate in relationships of mutual giving." This enables you to truly network quality relationships.

7. **Fearing Change.** This one is huge. When this dynamic shows up (and it does in most of us), we find ourselves looking for events around us to stay the same so we can feel secure. It's based on the illusion that

stability and security can be found in the changing world around us rather than within us. So, people don't want to change because they think that they can keep things the same all the time to feel safe.

When you're free of this dynamic, your attitude changes. You are likely to say, "Wow, I have no idea what's going to happen, but whatever it is, it's going to be a good surprise."

In my case, for the first twenty years of business, every January I would say to myself, "Oh gosh, I wonder where my next dollar is going to come from." I worried because the research I developed had a "shelf life" and I would have to identify new cutting-edge research and figure out first what to research and then how to market it. This sent me into panic mode, scrambling for solutions and not being very pleasant to be around until about March. However, after having the core dynamics "debugged" about six years ago, I found myself saying, "Oh gee, I wonder what cool things I'm going to be doing this year to increase my business. It's sure going to be interesting and fun to find out!" The result of this change of attitude and embracing of change was to double my revenues that first year and enjoy steady growth over the past five years. I see similar results for my clients. They may not double their revenues, but they definitely increase their bottom line and do it with a lot less stress.

8. **Playing it Safe.** This dynamic is particularly prevalent among women who are commonly taught to "be nice" and not make waves. So sometimes the glass ceiling can be self-imposed, negatively affecting their careers. It also affects men preparing for executive positions. Here, both men and women are limiting self-expression because they tend to hold themselves back in the fear of losing approval of others or that they'll be leaving others behind. It's based on the illusion that if they powerfully express themselves; they are going to be isolated. Many times people who could go well beyond their potential are afraid that if they really express themselves and do what they really want to do, their peers, their parents, or their family won't love them anymore. They'll be abandoned and they will feel lonely at the top. What they don't realize is that there are other people at the top and that they will make new friends.

Regrettably, playing it safe because of fear of isolation promotes mediocrity. We see this all the time in business. In the corporate environment there are often politics involved. Knowing how to express oneself in a politically charged environment adds to the challenge, but is possible. Thus, when this dynamic is removed, one can say, "I am fully self-expressed without fearing loss of love of others."

9. **Trying to Force an Outcome.** When this dynamic is operating, people feel compelled to make things happen. These folks are commonly known as control freaks. They want things done in a particular way or in a particular time frame—"my way or the highway." They mistakenly believe that they alone have control over what happens in their lives. When this dynamic is removed, they get a sense of themselves from the essential nature of who they are rather than from their actions or accomplishments. This is true particularly in leadership roles. Many leaders who have to lead and direct others make the mistake of thinking that they are the ones who have to do it, as opposed to setting the example and letting others take on their own responsibilities.

10. **Needing To Be Right.** What happens here is excluding others' perspectives. When this dynamic is present, we tend to over identify with our minds and think we have and need to have all of the answers. It comes from not recognizing the difference between thinking with our minds and knowing from our deepest level or our soul. When this dynamic is absent, we are free to continually be open to new ways of seeing things and increase our creativity. With that mindset, we start to look for greater possibilities that could lead to serendipitous results and creative breakthroughs, rather than narrowly focusing on a solution to one particular problem and never seeing beyond it.

11. **Biasing Reality.** Basically when this happens, we manufacture interpretations by unknowingly fabricating explanations. We get overly absorbed in trying to explain or interpret events, instead of recognizing things "are what they are." There *is* nothing to explain. This behavior is based on the illusion that everything is not perfect as it is. Our intellect gets in the way and tries to justify things instead of accepting them as they are. When this dynamic is absent, we tend to be in the flow and appreciate the present. From a business perspective, we learn to capitalize on a situation, rather than to fight it. Hence, we take the path of least resistance, which enables us to see opportunities and move forward.

12. **Overreacting To Circumstances.** When this is present, we become overly disturbed or distressed by what happens to others or ourselves. It interferes with our ability to maintain a strong sense of who we are under extreme conditions. This limits our ability to see things clearly and make informed decisions. We jump to conclusions by making erroneous assumptions. When this dynamic is removed, we feel a sense of balance or calmness, whether we are experiencing a joyful or painful event. This balance allows us to maintain perspective and not take things personally when business crises occur, allowing us to lead with resolve.

Once these twelve core dynamics (conditioned responses) are removed, it makes accomplishing a client's goals much easier. There is much less struggle. For example, if you fear change, how are you going to respond to a goal that requires significant change? By getting rid of the obstacle, then you can address the goal and create an action plan without the underlying resistance.

WRIGHT

Will you tell our readers how you test to make sure they are removed?

FRIED

I use something called "muscle response testing" and it is based on kinesiology. Let me give you a little background on that. Muscle response testing is a diagnostic technique that's valuable in many procedures and treatments. It was originally developed by a chiropractor. In fact, many books have been written on muscle response testing, including one written in 1995 by Dr. David R. Hawkins who is a medical doctor and psychiatrist. Dr. Hawkins previously coauthored a book on Ortho Molecular Psychiatry with Nobel prizewinner, Linus Palling.

This is how muscle response testing works. A practitioner gently pushes down on a client's arm, which is resisting a downward pressure. If we irritate the nervous system for a second, it will cause a temporary short circuit causing the testing arm to momentarily go weak (off). We can irritate the nervous system by touching a sensitive area of the body, a weakened reflex, or acupuncture point. It has been found to be about 90 percent accurate.

When I use it, however, I apply the same principles, but I use energy as my focus. There are thousands of instant reactions going on in the nervous system on a cellular and tissue level. But before I continue, I must ask you a question. Do you believe that everything in this world is made out of some form of energy?

WRIGHT

Yes. If we look under an electron microscope we can see molecules and atoms and they are constantly moving.

FRIED

Okay. So do you think our thoughts create energy?

WRIGHT

Yes. An EEG picks up brainwaves when tests are done on the brain. So, my answer is yes.

FRIED

Okay. So basically, when I talk to somebody and he or she makes a statement or expresses an intention, I can test whether the person truly believes in or resonates with that comment. For example, if I said to you, "Please extend your arm. I'm only going to take two fingers to press on your arm—don't let me push it down, but just meet my pressure and make it strong." Then I say, "Now, tell me that your name is David Wright." And you say, "My name is David Wright." Typically, the results will be that your arm will remain strong (on). If I say, "Say my name is Rick Springsteen." And you say, "My name is Rick Springsteen," your arm will go weak (off) because you don't believe that. It doesn't resonate with you.

When I remove a core dynamic, I test clients initially to see if the core dynamic is present. For example, if I say to a client, "I want you to say, 'I always live in the present,'" and the person's arm goes down (off), this tells me that he or she doesn't believe that statement. This then leads to a discussion. We bring all the issues up related to that core dynamic so the client is very conscious of his or her thoughts about it. The objective is to bring these energy thought wave patterns within the client's sphere. Once that is complete, I use a piece of equipment called a Wavemaker* to debug the core dynamic. The Wavemaker uses inverse wave technology or wave interference and deletes the energy patterns associated with those thoughts.

Here's how it works. Have you ever heard of noise canceling earphones?

WRIGHT

Yes.

FRIED

Noise canceling headsets use a built-in microphone to pick up background noise and run the waveform of the noise through circuitry designed to invert it. Both the mirror image of the noise and the original noise are sent back to the ear simultaneously. This process results in completely eliminating the noise. You simply don't hear it. It doesn't just shield the ears from the noise—it actually takes the energy pattern of the noise and wipes it out by producing its own electronic mirror image. This physics principle is termed "wave interference."

So in the case I mentioned earlier, when I am ready to debug the core dynamic, I have the client hold onto two terminals and we do the wave interference. One terminal is the input that picks up and scans the person's body of the energy wave pattern of that thought. The other one sends back the inverse or canceling pattern. After a prescribed period of time, the particular core dynamic is debugged. To insure this, I muscle test the client and I have him or her repeat the same statement: "I always live in the present." When I do, I won't be able to move his or her arm down; it will be strong.

Every time I do this, David, it amazes me. I'm a person who tends to be very scientific; the first time I was introduced to this I thought, "Yeah, right!" until I had it done to me and saw it happen. And the interesting thing is, once these core dynamics are removed, then the person can progress more easily, thus requiring less practice and coaching. Here, we've basically kicked the legs out from under obstacles that stand in the way.

WRIGHT

I was introduced to kinesiology many years ago and like you, I was just dumbfounded by it. It's so simple it can be demonstrated by anyone, but most people I demonstrate it to think it's like a parlor game. There is nothing mystical or magical about it. I remember the first time I did it. A gentleman let me hold a sealed envelope and he tested my muscle by pushing down on my arm, but he could put it down with one finger. Then, he gave me another envelope and he could almost chin up on my arm, it was so strong.

FRIED

What was in the envelope? Do you know?

WRIGHT

Sugar was in the first and nuts were in the second.

FRIED

In other words, your body was definitely weakened by sugar and it was fine with nuts. Now, if you had been allergic to nuts, it would've gone down.

WRIGHT

You could almost test any food that is good or bad for you that way. It was so fascinating, as you said. On me it worked 100 percent of the time.

Now let me ask you, once you've cleared out all major obstacles through this testing, then can you actually start working on the goals?

FRIED

Absolutely. Initially, I have the client list all the goals that he or she wants to work on. Then we will muscle test to determine which goals should be worked on first. I'll typically say, "Which goal would you like to work on first? Then, let's test it and find out if it's really the goal that you truly want to work on. Sometimes the goal you choose is one that you think is logical for you to work on because someone else wants you to, but is not necessarily the one that best for you." Typically, if the client works on the goal indicated by his or her body's signals, subsequent goals are easier to accomplish. This process amazes me each and every time that I do it. It's a very thrilling and satisfying approach.

Now, I do have one caveat. After I clear out the core dynamics, sometimes there are deeper issues that come up. The analogy I like to use is cleaning your house. Let's say your house is very dirty and you hire a cleaning person to come in. The cleaning person cleans the whole house and all of a sudden it just looks sparkling. That's like clearing out the twelve core dynamics. As you walk around the house and you look around, you are very pleased. Then you happen to run your finger along the windowsill and notice that there is some dust. Now, you wouldn't have even noticed the dust if the housekeeper hadn't cleared everything else away first for you to see it. So we still have some "dust bunnies" that might surface because they were so hidden by all the stuff that was on top of them and they couldn't be noticed. We clear the dust bunnies in a similar way with the Wave-maker and muscle checking.

Remember, this process does not replace coaching. It supplements it, making your coaching faster and more effective. Generally, I can help a client achieve significant results within four months—at the most six—on engagements that would typically take a year to two. It's just faster. Now, if a client doesn't want to go down this route, that's fine with me, it is a matter of choice. I'll go the traditional route only, but I know the blended strategy just speeds up the process. It's up to the clients and their comfort level.

WRIGHT

Will you give our readers some examples of clients you have helped?

FRIED

I'm going to give you a golfing example. My work is confidential but this client has given me permission to share her story. Susie had a desire to become a scratch golfer and play with others whose skill level was higher than hers. We talked about what was preventing her from doing this. She said to me that she had learned to play golf at age fifty when her sister bought her a set of clubs for her birthday. Her sister, a skilled golfer and always the top player at her country club, taught Susie how to play. While instructing Susie, her sister was somewhat impatient and would say things like, "Now be sure you're ready. Don't take too much time to set up or people aren't going to want to play with you." Every time Susie stepped up to the tee, she would hear her sister's scolding voice in her head, which would make her very nervous and she would blow the shot.

We nailed down which core dynamics were operating through a series of questions and discussion followed by muscle checking. For example, we determined one of the core dynamics present was *playing it safe*. She feared that if she did it her own way and fully expressed herself that she would upset her sister and cause a rift. So we removed that core dynamic in this particular instance along with another related one.

Then something really unusual happened. The very next day, Susie called me elated. "You're not going to believe this. I went to the country club and I was grouped with people I had never played with before and they were all better players. We not only won the round, but I also never heard my sister's voice in my head the entire time I played!" And, she has never heard it since!

Several weeks later, she called me again—I'll never forget—and said, "Here is one for the record books. I got a hole-in-one!"

After congratulating her I said, "I'll bet your game fell apart right after that, right?"

She sighed, "Well, yeah."

The hole-in-one was lucky and then she got so excited she couldn't concentrate for the remainder of the game. We probably should have worked on *overreacting to circumstances* in that initial session. But who knew she would get a hole-in-one!

WRIGHT

This really is fascinating stuff. I really appreciate all the time you've taken with me this morning to answer these questions. I always enjoy talking with you. I always learn a lot. I can hear your passion for your subject even as we talk.

FRIED

Well, as I say, I'm always amazed at how well this works. It's like the radio—I know sounds come through the radio and I'm not exactly sure how it works, but it works. That's all I can tell you.

WRIGHT

Even stranger, how do pictures fly through the air, bounce off satellites and into television?

FRIED

I know I went out on a limb today to talk about something that was very far out there. It would be interesting to discover which readers of this book can embrace thinking about things in a slightly different way. But, I challenge the doubters who say if you can't see it or feel it, it can't be. I'd ask them to think about viruses and bacteria. Before the microscope was invented, we never would have believed that they existed and could affect us.

WRIGHT

Maybe you went out on a limb for a lot of people, but you are preaching to the choir with me. I don't use it as you do, but I certainly believe in it. I wish I could discipline myself to use it more often. In any event, I'm sure that our readers are going to get a lot out of this chapter. I really sincerely appreciate your doing it.

FRIED

Well, I've kept a pretty low profile on this until now. I've been using it for about five years with select clients. But, as you know, timing is everything. I think that there are more people ready to hear this today, especially with recent interest in the laws of attraction discussed in *The Secret*. It's my understanding the book sold more than six million copies and was on *The*

York Times' best-sellers list for over eighty weeks. These concepts have even reached mainstream television like *The Oprah Winfrey Show.* So, it was my pleasure to share this. I know it works because I've helped many people succeed.

WRIGHT

Today we have been talking with Dr. Elizabeth Fried. She is an executive coach. She is also an author and a consultant. She speaks to audiences on topics such as 360 feedback, employee engagement, and coaching. As we have found out here today, I think she knows what she is talking about.

Thank you so much, Elizabeth, for being with us today on *Coaching for Success.*

FRIED

I've enjoyed our time together, David and am glad to have had a forum to discuss this exciting new approach.

About the Author

Dr. N. Elizabeth Fried, author, consultant, and executive coach, is president of N. E. Fried and Associates, Inc. For the past twenty-five years, her firm has served more than fifteen hundred clients worldwide. A vibrant, entertaining, and informative speaker, she is frequently invited to speak on such topics as 360 feedback, employee engagement, and coaching. Her first book, *Outrageous Conduct: Bizarre Behavior at Work,* was a Society of Human Resource Management best seller, followed by its sequel, *Sex, Laws, and Stereotypes.* Her work has been quoted in the *Wall Street Journal, USA Today, The New York Times, The Chicago Tribune, Washington Post, US News and World Report, MS, Business Week,* and *FORTUNE Magazine.* She has also been a featured guest on over one hundred radio and television broadcasts. TheLearningEngine.org, MyExecutiveCoach.net, and Intermediaries Speakers Bureau are divisions of the firm.

N. Elizabeth Fried, PhD

7564 Romeria St.
Carlsbad, CA 92009
760.633.4444
elizabeth@TheLearningEngine.org
www.TheLearningEngine.org
www.MyExecutiveCoach.net

Chapter 5

Frumi Rachel Barr
MBA, Ph. D.

COMMUNICATION:

A CORNERSTONE FOR

SUCCESS

THE INTERVIEW

DAVID WRIGHT (WRIGHT)

Today we're talking with Frumi Rachel Barr. Frumi is a catalyst for change, and she is an experienced business advisor, mentor, and leadership coach. She works with senior leaders and their teams to facilitate their ability to leverage their strengths, address critical development challenges, manage conflict, and achieve results in their business and organizational objectives. She has had a distinguished career history as an entrepreneur and financial executive. Her experience and expertise as both CEO and CFO provides responsive and collaborative support to executives in a wide array of companies and industries including manufacturing, service industries, and direct marketing. It is this unique blend of practical, theoretical, and strategic skills that makes the work Frumi does quite unique among business advisors and coaches. Indeed, when clients work with Frumi they can expect a positive "Frunami." Leaders spend focused attention on their financial results, on both internal and external communication, and on alignment between their business and personal goals. Frumi inspires leaders to rediscover the strengths and values that energize them so that they in turn can renew their colleagues, employees, and business operations.

She is a past President of the National Board of the Professional Coaches and Mentors Association. She serves on the Board of Directors for Web Wise Kids, an organization that empowers children to protect themselves from online predators, and she serves on the Board of Directors of Hope University. She currently mentorship director for the International Coach Federation (ICF) Orange County Chapter.

After twenty-five years in the business world, Frumi earned a master's degree in Business Administration from California State University at Fullerton and her doctorate in Business Administration. Her firsthand business acumen and formal business studies are complimented by her training as a business coach through the Hudson Institute of Santa Barbara.

Frumi, welcome to *Coaching for Success.*

FRUMI BARR (BARR)

Thank you, David.

WRIGHT

So what makes the area of communication so fascinating to you and your coaching engagements?

BARR

The quality of the conversations that people have is directly related to the level of results that they achieve. Probably the most important element of communicating with others is understanding what their perspectives are, so listening, therefore, becomes almost more important than speaking.

In order to listen well it's also important to know how to ask questions. You know, David, one of my strengths is being a continuous learner. I write book notes on many topics and I share these book notes with clients and colleagues monthly. They give me the knowledge to not only coach my clients but also to give them a lot of resources to draw on. So I tend to refer to many authors and books when I talk to interviewers or when I talk to my clients.

One of my favorite books—one of the most transformational books that I've shared with clients—is a book called, *Change Your Questions, Change Your Life,* by Marilee Adams. We all think in questions and then we take an action. As a result of our action, then we create certain results so it stands to reason that if we ask better and more insightful questions, we'll actually get better results.

When I shared this particular book with one of my clients she got so excited about it that she suggested purchasing ten or fifteen books for her management team. Before I knew it, this way of thinking had permeated the whole organization. We actually created "question thinking" with the board; the whole organization ended up with a common language and started to achieve different results. This transformational way of thinking was very exciting.

WRIGHT

Are there certain themes or communication issues that arise most often in the companies and the executives you coach?

BARR

I would say that there are three major themes that show up. The first one is not talking about the things that matter to them most; people seem to skirt around the issues. They're so busy "doing" that they don't take a step back to actually take the time to do the thinking that will create change and better results. I try to have my clients focus by asking the following question: "What is the conversation you are not having and what is the one thing you need to do to actually change things?" That's why they call me "the catalyst for change." I show up with dynamite and Band-Aids and everything changes.

The second major issue is that there is an avoidance of conflict in almost every company. People seem to think that the very word "conflict" always dredges up thoughts of arguments. In truth, conflict handled well will make people cooperate at a higher level and will create better results. If everyone just nods their head when someone makes a suggestion, how would we know if they have arrived at the best possible solution for any given problem? But people are afraid to speak up and they are afraid to be seen as ornery and not cooperative; as a result, most people really avoid conflict.

The third thing that comes up, believe it or not, is the fact that people try to avoid conversations altogether by using e-mail as a preferred method of communication. Although it's the easiest form of communication, using e-mail often causes and escalates arguments. This is because you can't hear the tone of someone's voice and it is easy to create your own story rather than focus on facts.

Those are the three major themes.

WRIGHT

Do you find that executives and management teams have the right conversations?

BARR

Very often I find that team meetings are about reporting activities and not about what really matters and what is critical to address in the corporation. So when I show up, I usually change the whole nature of the way meetings are handled.

I suggest that people create very thoughtful agendas where they do their reporting in terms of highlights. They might say, "Here are the three headlines of what is going on in my particular department, and here's the conversation that I would like to have in the meeting." This changes the texture of the meeting because instead of just reporting, they actually start to talk about what is important to them or what they're challenged with.

I feel that every team is like a brain trust at the table. If people don't create the opportunities to have conversations instead of reporting, they're really not taking advantage of the brains and the smart people who are with them. When they start to look at meetings in this way, they start to catch on that maybe they can have a more strategic use of the time spent in meetings.

Second of all, though, there needs to be a strong degree of trust in the group in order for teams to share well. Very often I find that there needs to be some kind of team refresher—a renewal for the team so they can start sharing on a higher level. Also, many companies are led by leaders who have strong technical skills, but who haven't really learned how to lead others. They would be well served to start changing their conversations using more of a questioning approach so that they can hear what their followers and their executive teams have to say. No executive with a team at hand needs to feel that he or she is totally alone in solving problems.

WRIGHT

What team subject matters and/or issues are team members afraid to discuss?

BARR

They tend to avoid any subject that may be difficult or might create conflict. So for example, if they have a difference of opinion or if they think that someone isn't handling their own management team well, they won't say anything, they'll just skirt around it. The most difficult subject to address, however, is how to keep others accountable for achieving the results that they project. I see this most often in budget season, and you know that everybody struggles with creating a budget. Very often they don't address what wasn't achieved last year; they just skirt the issue because it's a tough one to discuss.

WRIGHT

So how do you "mine for conflict"?

BARR

Well, conflict is a word that I just love because I think that in a meeting, you can have a much richer discussion if there is conflict. I listen for opportunities with the mindset that there will be a better outcome if everyone at the table contributes their real perspective. So if someone makes a comment and I'm present, then I will challenge him or her to expand on it—to explain it. I'll ask other people what their perspectives are. There has to be someone at the table who is willing to have these difficult conversations and willing to mine for the conflict.

When you hear items creating conflict, jump on the opportunity for a juicy conversation and ask the insightful questions. Welcome everyone's point of view and make them feel heard. If the leader is not conflict averse then it would be great if he or she would be the one to do that. Often, however, because the leader hasn't taken leadership courses, it's the coach who has to come in and help the leader have success in mining for conflict so that he or she feels comfortable doing it.

WRIGHT

So you actually start the conversation and people are more active after you've shown the first question.

BARR

That's exactly right—I lead the way. I model how it would work to mine for conflict and this is often a conversation that I have with the leader before the meeting starts. I'll say, "I'm going to mine for conflict in this meeting. I'd like your support in doing that, and when you see how I do it, you'll start to feel comfortable doing it yourself." And that's what happens.

WRIGHT

I understand that you're also a certified mediator. How does that mesh with your coaching practice?

BARR

Because I love mining for conflict, and because someone at the table has to be comfortable with the prospect of creating conflict, my mediation certification has given me both the confidence and the skills to be that person.

In my role I create a safe environment and focus on the outcomes to keep people on track. We jointly create an outcome that we want to reach and then it's easier to deal with conflict because they're focusing on the outcome, not the discomfort of being in that messy middle space. I usually discuss listening for common ground, and set up the listening for them—for each other—and I create a safe place.

I have a favorite methodology when people are in conflict. I help them listen carefully to the person speaking and then feed back what they think they heard the person say. If they're not correct, the person has an opportunity to say something like, "No, that's not quite what I meant." So the person has an opportunity to try another way to present his or her thoughts. This process goes back and forth like a ping-pong ball until both speaker and those listening "get it." What happens then is that everyone feels validated. The person speaking feels validated because he or she feels the message has been understood. That shows a great deal of respect, and even that will help simmer down the conflict and achieve a better result.

The second person (or the people in the meeting) has a degree of satisfaction of hearing the issue more clearly.

WRIGHT

That was a technique used in the '70s, '80s, and I guess into the '90s. It is still done in marital counseling.

BARR

Right. As a matter of fact, one of my favorite books is *Getting the Love You Want,* by Harville Hendricks. It's a mirroring technique that I first learned from his books, but it works perfectly in corporations. I mean, conversation is conversation, and they're all about relationships. So creating that safe place for two people or a team to have a good conversation really furthers the momentum.

WRIGHT

Do they stay on track? Is that what you want or do you want more conversation?

BARR

I want more conversation, but I want people to really hear each other and understand each other because that creates trust and a feeling of safety. With trust and safety, success is more often a result that will encourage them to do it again and again.

WRIGHT

So what can people do to achieve the desired outcome of a conversation?

BARR

Well, I think that when people prepare and consider what the desired outcome is that they're looking for, then they can think of what needs to be presented to get there. I don't suggest rushing into a conversation without thinking before opening your mouth. Often, I find myself telling people how important it is to slow down in order to speed up. Sometimes you have to allow yourself to "sit in the question," as I call it; you can't just jump into it. So you have to prepare, you have to think, you have to increase the time (this is a Stephen Covey thing) between the stimulus and the response. You don't have to fire back a response; you can sit in the question and ask yourself: Am I addressing the right issue? Is this what I want to talk about?

At every juncture, when you do start the conversation, you have to consider if you're keeping the conversation safe. One of the best ways I think there is to keep it safe is, first of all, to respect the person, even if you don't respect the person. For the sake of the conversation you have to respect the person. Further, stay in a state of curiosity rather than judgment, because when you're curious about someone and you say to him or her, "I'm curious about why you would do that," it creates an atmosphere of safety. It doesn't sound judgmental when you're curious.

WRIGHT

Does the conversation between people generally get personal or just every once in a while?

BARR

Unfortunately, too many times it does become personal. That's exactly when people start to lose trust and they start to lose faith in the process, so it's important to step in. For example, let's say we're in a team meeting, and I say, "This is getting personal and I don't think it needs to be. Let's try to change our questions and stay with being curious." So it's okay to jump in there and help them correct themselves. That in itself is training.

WRIGHT

Is there a formula or methodology that you recommend to your clients that assures desired outcomes?

BARR

Having read numerous conversation books such as *Difficult Conversations, Fierce Conversations, Crucial Conversations,* I can say that they're all wonderful and they're all actually very similar. The one I like the best is by Patterson, Grenny, McMillan, and Switzler and is titled, *Crucial Confrontations: Tools for Resolving Broken Promises, Violated Expectations, and Bad Behavior.* This book shares a beautiful model because it allows you first to ask yourself: What is the situation? What should I be talking about? What is the real issue? Then it moves into: Should I have the conversation. What happens if I do? What happens if I don't? So when you start the conversation, decide what the issue is.

If you should start the conversation, the next thing is to master the stories and make sure you're just working on the facts and not on the story about the facts.

The next step is to confront someone with safety—to describe the gap between what the person said he or she would do and what the person did do. So if you're holding someone accountable and the person said he or she would prepare something for you by Wednesday at noon and he or she let you down, then you begin with that.

The next step is to also find out if it's a question of whether the person is motivated to the desired task and whether the person actually has the skills to do what was promised. If you recognize that the individual doesn't have the skills, then you need to make it easy for the person.

And finally, the last thing is to move into action, create a plan, and follow up on the plan. Very often people don't have a model for having a conversation. When you teach them a model it becomes very simple because then they start to think of it in steps. They can move in and out of the conversation and create safety. The "Crucial Confrontation" model is indeed my favorite model and it's very effective.

WRIGHT

So how can we use conversations that count to create a detailed plan of action?

BARR

The key is to never leave an important conversation without action steps or a plan for follow-up. Most of the time, when you have a serious conversation with someone and you don't get the results that you want, it's usually because you failed to determine who's going to follow up and when. It's always important to end a meeting with saying, "Okay, what are the action steps and who is going to follow up?" If you are very certain that the person designated can handle it then you can say, "Let's have this ready by Wednesday at noon." If you're not sure about the skills, then in order to have the right results you really have to say to the person, "I'm going to call you on Monday to see if there's anything that's in your way." You might say, "Is there any help that you need to resolve this so we can have it by Wednesday at noon?"

When people don't take the steps to create a concrete plan of action, the result is often not as stellar as you want. You can see that people go to a lot of trouble to set up a conversation. If they forget to take this crucial step, then they will find themselves repeating the disappointment over and over again. That's another way people lose trust with each other—not doing what they say they're going to do and following up. You can't trust a person who does that—the whole relationship is at risk.

WRIGHT

Let me ask you about one of my pet issues, and maybe I can get some firsthand knowledge myself. How does technology such as e-mail affect communication in companies?

BARR

It's interesting that it's your pet peeve because it's definitely my pet peeve as well. What I so often see in companies is that two people can be sitting in the office next to each other and instead of standing up and walking in to the office and looking at a co-worker, the person fires off an e-mail "conversation." Both have missed the opportunity to have an eyeball-to-eyeball conversation and observe each other's body language. Instead, they go back and forth with e-mail, very often creating misunderstandings and having the e-mail conversation escalate into an argument.

Now, some people will defend this position by saying, "Well, I want to have an e-mail trail—I want to have it all in writing." But essentially, the wrong things are in writing because they could have resolved all of this and it would have taken far less time and energy to just pick up the phone or visit in person. Very often, when I hear people talking about conflict, what they're talking about is something that was developed through a string of e-mails. When I ask, "Well, why didn't you pick up the phone?" it's as though a light bulb goes on and I get a response like, "Uh, I don't know." People have forgotten that there are other ways to do business.

You may have gathered that for me there's nothing like a conversation. There's nothing like looking into the eyes of other people you're talking with, observing body language, and seeing when they feel safe or when they feel threatened. Individuals should only use e-mail for confirming things for follow-up, such as, "Here's what we agreed to do. Let me know if I'm wrong," and setting up appointments. Even then, how many times does an e-mail bounce back and forth when you're trying to set a meeting? It could take like six iterations. It doesn't make any sense to not look at the calendar while you're on the phone with the person. So I find that more and more people are relying on their technology and less and less on their relationships. I think that this is a disappointing route for communication to take.

WRIGHT

I almost laughed when you were talking about keeping a trail; I get that a lot. We've got to have everything documented as if we're going to court. I've been in this particular business now eighteen years and I've never sued anyone in that whole time, so I really don't need a trail. But I also experience these kinds of feelings on the telephone. I feel that I know when I'm being threatened—I feel all kinds of feelings when I can hear the voice as well. Do you feel that way?

BARR

I am sure you know that many coaches (and I'm one of them) do a lot of coaching by phone. You develop a very finely tuned ear. I'm sure you do when you interview people. You get a finely tuned ear for what people are feeling. You know when they feel excitement, and if they're feeling threatened, as well as their energy level. Sometimes it's interesting that people can also misunderstand messages that are left on voice mail.

I had one client call me one day. He was very up in arms about a voice mail he received. I suggested that he play it to me. I listened to it and I said, "Isn't that strange. I don't hear what you're hearing. Here's what I'm hearing. Why don't you just walk around the corner into this person's office and have a conversation?"

I think that when you get very used to e-mail it also sets you up to get very used to voice mail and not taking those steps to the other office. When he actually went in and had the conversation, it was a totally different conversation than he would have had if he hadn't seen some other options of what the person was saying in the voice mail.

WRIGHT

So what haven't I asked you that you would like to share with our readers and our listeners?

BARR

Well three things: First of all, I have one book that is out on the market called *Confessions of a Resilient Entrepreneur: Persevering to Success.* The second thing is that I am very excited about my next adventure. I am hoping to put together a series called *Knowledge of the Masters,* which would be a compilation of all the book notes that I write, which are very comprehensive. My book notes are like "CliffsNotes" and I'm hoping to group them into themes and make them available for all those very overwhelmed people who are racing from meeting to meeting, airport to airport, so they can read the knowledge of the masters. Perhaps reading the summaries will whet their appetite for reading the full book; that's my current passion.

Thirdly, The Forum for CFOs is a new offering that I am really excited about. It is a chance for CFOs to continue to develop themselves within a peer group. The Forum offers opportunities to share issues, to discuss case studies, and to learn from each other. Featured experts discuss subjects that the participating CFOs choose to hear about. We use a proven process for accelerating personal and business results to ensure a strong ROI for participation.

WRIGHT

Well, you can put me on the list for the notes series. I met a fellow back in the '70s who was frustrated that he couldn't read as much as he would like. He had to read all kinds of materials to keep up in his industry. I asked him, "So how does it make you feel?" He said, "I feel like I'm sitting in front of a fireplug—the water's coming at me full force and I'm drinking with a straw!"

BARR

That's quite a vision isn't it?

WRIGHT

I've never forgotten it. I feel that way quite often, so I'm waiting for your compilation book to come out.

BARR

If you get a chance, go to my Web site: www.clarityandresults.com. There are about one hundred and twenty sets of book notes. Help yourself.

WRIGHT

What a pleasure it was to talk with you today and how thankful I am that you took all this time to answer these questions for me. I have learned a lot here today and I am sure that our readers will as well.

BARR

Thank you, David. It was my pleasure.

WRIGHT

Today we've been talking with Frumi Rachel Barr, who is called "the catalyst for change." She is an experienced business advisor, mentor, and leadership coach. She works with leaders and their teams helping them to leverage their strengths and address critical development challenges to manage conflict and achieve results in their business and in their organizational objectives.

Frumi, thank you so much for being with us today on *Coaching for Success.*

BARR

Thank you so much, David.

About the Author

She is a past President of the National Board of the Professional Coaches and Mentors Association. She serves on the Board of Directors for Web Wise Kids, an organization that empowers children to protect themselves from online predators, and she serves on the Board of Directors of Hope University. She currently mentorship director for the International Coach Federation (ICF) Orange County Chapter.

After twenty-five years in the business world, Frumi earned a master's degree in Business Administration from California State University in Fullerton, and her doctorate in Business Communications. Her firsthand business acumen and formal business studies are complemented by her training as a business coach, through the Hudson Institute of Santa Barbara. She holds multiple certifications including Barr-ON EQ-I, Conflict Resolution and Mediation, Group Coaching and Virtual Facilitation.

FRUMI RACHEL BARR, MBA, PHD
2711 Hillside Drive
Newport Beach
949.729.1577
ceocoach@frumi.com
www.clarityandresults.com

Chapter 6

David Brookmire

THE INTERVIEW

DAVID WRIGHT (WRIGHT)

Today we're talking with David Brookmire. Dave Brookmire is a seasoned executive advisor and recognized authority on organizational, team, and executive leadership effectiveness. An expert in organizational psychology, Dave's experience in business consulting is extensive, spanning more than thirty years of providing business strategy, expansion, and process enhancement solutions to global corporations and top-level executives.

His approach to client service combines business acumen with expertise in organizational effectiveness and optimizing human capital. Throughout his career, Dave's strategies have directly contributed to numerous measurable benefits on behalf of his clients in the areas of global HR effectiveness, international expansion and merger success, talent and executive leadership development, and succession planning for business continuity.

In addition to his client service career, David is a recognized speaker on executive performance improvement and business effectiveness topics. His national speaking engagements cover numerous in-demand business concepts, including "Designing a High Quality M&A Process that Delivers" and "Managing and Leading High Impact Executive Coaching in Your Organization." His cutting-edge presentations on business strategy and human resource improvement have been presented to diverse audiences ranging from Wall Street analysts to corporate board members.

In a nutshell, David, how does your organization define executive coaching?

DAVID BROOKMIRE (BROOKMIRE)

Coaching is often incorrectly viewed by corporate leaders as a subjective or amorphous process. But the science of professional coaching is just that— a science. It is standards- and outcomes-based, and it is delivered by a practitioner with professional credentials.

Quality executive coaching enables businesses to retain long-term skills and abilities for efficiency and continuity, and protect themselves from process interruption or corporate level failures in the event of unexpected or large-scale transitions, including workforce growth periods, executive succession planning and execution, merger and acquisitions, and the loss of expertise of effective leadership in high profile, influential positions.

According to our model, a successful coaching relationship will include five key elements:

- A qualified coach
- A defined process
- Links to the organization's strategic plan
- Quality assurance
- Measurement of impact and results

Built on this foundation, effective coaching programs help top-level leadership answer crucial questions about business operations, sustainability, and scalability, and they help each business develop a strong foundation for long-term growth and viability, independent of economic or other external conditions. Some of these questions include:

- ❖ Do your senior leaders consistently meet—better yet, exceed— your company's strategic goals?
- ❖ What leadership skills are required to meet your company's strategic goals?
- ❖ How do your leadership skills stack up against international leadership best practices?
- ❖ How do you identify high-potential employees? Who are they?

❖ How do you prepare your high-potentials to move to the next level?

❖ What skills do your high-potentials need to develop in order to advance within your organization and contribute to its growth?

WRIGHT

Why is executive coaching important to businesses, especially in the current economy?

BROOKMIRE

Effective executive coaching has become a well-accepted method for developing leaders. More and more companies are deploying executive coaching either as a standalone method or integrated with the company's leadership development processes. When deployed with the five key elements outlined above it helps ensure that the company achieves the goals set out for the process. On an overall basis, effective executive coaching can improve the skills and performance of leaders, and when these are in the most critical or salient areas of the job, coaching leads to improved productivity, employee engagement, and customer satisfaction.

A few specific examples of where executive coaching can have a significant impact should be helpful. As background, senior leaders are averaging less and less tenure in their roles. There are several key reasons for this, including buyouts, mergers, failure to perform, and talent shortages. Combined with more and more senior transitions is significant research identifying large failure rates in transitions of 40 percent to 50 percent. ("Failure" is defined here as failing to meet the expectations in expected timeframes or losing one's job).

An effective application of executive coaching is New Leader Assimilation Coaching, which focuses on helping the newly appointed leader in succeeding and in coming up to full performance in shorter periods of time than without coaching. This method of coaching applies the core principals of effective coaching with research on best practices found to facilitate the transition for senior leaders.

Another specific application of effective executive coaching is when the method is integrated with the development process for high potentials that are being prepared to assume roles of greater responsibility in the future. In these cases, we identify the key competencies essential for success at the next levels of the organization, assess the executive against these profiles, compare him or her to a group of outstanding leaders, and coach with development goals documented in the plans.

What we see in most companies of all sizes is the lack of focus on the transfer of knowledge from one executive to another as transitions occur. Often the company has no real notice, and the executive resigns or is terminated. At other times, there is a planned event—retirement, transfer, and promotion—that can be controlled and will allow for more effective knowledge transfer to occur. Even in the latter situations, many companies do not capture the outgoing knowledge that leaves when the key employee leaves. Executive coaching, combined with effective knowledge transfer ensures that key expertise and core competencies are retained in the company, even after transitions occur.

One helpful way for this to happen is to provide for overlap between the outgoing and incoming executive so that there is time to transfer the knowledge. Executive coaching can facilitate the capture of knowledge by working with the incoming and outgoing executives. Without effective executive coaching and emphasis on this transition, efficiency is lost, productivity suffers, turnover can occur with defections of team members, and lots of other negative outcomes may occur.

We have termed this specific vulnerability of companies, "the knowledge gap." Some refer to it as "the brain drain." By not dealing effectively with the knowledge gap, companies stand to lose valuable time, knowledge, skills, relationships, and other key components that create weaknesses, which over time can be exploited by the competition. Companies that proactively understand and attack this problem will be able to prevent the valuable loss of intellectual capital, especially as aging workers start to leave the workforce in significantly large numbers.

WRIGHT

What is the knowledge gap that exists in organizations and why is it relevant now?

BROOKMIRE

The knowledge gap is the intellectual capital leaving a company minus the intellectual capital retained in the business. Included in this area are the knowledge, experience, skills, judgment, and wisdom that reside with the people involved in the transitions. We believe that this intellectual capital has a direct impact on quality of service, profitability, sustainability, client relationships, and operational excellence.

While this applies to any company and any transition, what we really focus on is the knowledge gap occurring at the top of the organization in key technical, leadership, and administrative roles. The reason for this focus has to do with the vast numbers of Baby Boomers in the fifty-year-old and up range that will be retiring over the next five years. This will impact different sectors and industries in different ways. For example, a study last year reported that 26 percent of the public sector survey respondents have 25 percent to 50 percent of their workforce at retirement eligible age.

According to the U.S. Census, approximately 80 million Baby Boomers are now between forty-five to sixty-three years old. In five years they will start leaving the workforce in record numbers. We find that organizations are not dealing with this impending knowledge gap in consistent and systemic ways.

WRIGHT

Why is this issue such a critical business imperative for organizations to address?

BROOKMIRE

I have been dealing with knowledge gaps during my entire career as a senior HR leader in companies dealing with succession planning and transitions. The problem has always been around, but is becoming heightened now with the aging workforce, and growing C-level terminations and failure rates.

The knowledge gap has significant business sustainability implications. What if 25 to 50 percent of your most senior technical and leadership positions opened due to retirement in the next three to five years? Are you prepared?

Think about how that would impact your business. How long would it take to replace talent and get newly hired or promoted people up to speed? In addition to the technical knowledge of their positions, employees retain institutional knowledge, including how things work, what the informal network is to get things done, history of clients, and processes. Employees also have relationships with vendors, clients, and employees; they also know the most efficient way to get things done and they have goodwill. Replacing these skill sets and knowledge pools takes time, coaching, training, the right skills, and experience for the successors. Anytime someone leaves the organization there is a knowledge gap. The severity of the gap is a function of the level and tenure of the person leaving. If a company is not prepared for this eventuality, business disruptions will occur that could otherwise be prevented with careful planning and training.

WRIGHT

What challenges do organizations face when dealing with the knowledge gap?

BROOKMIRE

The first challenge is getting management's attention and convincing them that this is a real and pending issue. A 2007 study conducted by Career Innovation found that less than 15 percent of senior managers and less than 25 percent of HR managers were making large investments in time and resources to address this issue.

The second challenge is to ensure that organizations have the right data to forecast and profile their workforce and model these demographics into the future. Many mid to small sized firms do not invest time and resources into what has traditionally been called "human resources planning."

The third challenge is the mindset and cultural changes that need to occur as the older workers become more critical to business continuity. For the past century, everything was set up to help ease older workers out by age sixty to sixty-five. While that may be the case in this century, there needs to be some radical adjustments made to reshape the mindsets and cultures of companies around these transitions. The "gold watch" after thirty years is no longer enough planning for a business to ensure that it has adequately planned for large numbers of employees retiring.

The fourth challenge has to do with the way organizations are set up to function during business as usual. Every aspect is geared around this expectation of retirement—recruiting, retention, organization structure, mentoring, total rewards, policies, and processes. For retiring employees to want to stay engaged and helpful, organizations have to change a number of structural and process components for a smooth transition.

WRIGHT

How do you use executive coaching to help organizations with the knowledge gap?

BROOKMIRE

We find vast differences in the utilization of executive coaching with respect to developing leaders. Much of what we see in companies are executive coaches working with leaders independent of any set of strategic plans, leadership competencies, succession plans, or consistent processes. Executive coaching in itself is not the single most effective method for developing leaders. It is optimal when it is a part of an integrated system for developing leaders. In such systems, coaching is used to help executives apply new behaviors, tools, and concepts, and an experienced professional serves as an objective third party.

We have an integrated system for leadership development that embeds executive coaching as one of several leadership development techniques. This focused coaching toward the critical competencies required to achieve the strategic goals provides an effective method to help executives develop leadership on the job.

Our approach shows that:

- Executive coaching can be deployed toward the development of executives to prepare them for increased responsibility and to help them excel with increased responsibility. Done right, with the right coaches, the results of development can be powerful.
- Executive coaching can accelerate the transition of executives into new responsibilities, preventing failure and speeding up successful mastery. With the right coach and a one-hundred-day plan, this introductory period can be very efficient and effective, saving the organization time and valuable opportunity costs.
- Deploying coaching in an organization can be hugely helpful toward bridging the knowledge gap, but can also be very ineffective if not carefully implemented and monitored. There are countless times where companies bring in different coaches, all with their own assessments, competency models, beliefs, values, etc., that may or may not match what the organization needs or wants.

WRIGHT

How can organizations get started identifying their internal coaching needs?

BROOKMIRE

For companies to identify and address the knowledge gap within their organization, we recommend the following process:

- Determine the gap between what is needed and what you project to have.
- Get senior management buy-in.
- Create a sense of urgency to address the gaps.
- For the knowledge gap assessment, do the demographics for the senior most levels over the next five years. Look at historical turnover rates, retirements, and planned new openings that can result in key openings.
- Identify the competencies, knowledge, and experiences required in the next five years to achieve the strategic goals and vision.
- Objectively and accurately assess the backup for these key roles. Where there are shortages, do some strategic sourcing of talent. Where you have internal high potentials, create a system of leadership development.
- Action your development. Move it from the classroom to the real world. Utilize a variety of learning and development techniques, including 360 assessment, executive coaching, action learning, and job changes.

WRIGHT

In addition to executive coaching programs, what can organizations do to effectively address the knowledge gap?

BROOKMIRE

There are several areas I recommend addressing that tie into coaching and help in these organizational transitions. My focus for the rest of the interview will be on *developing a system for an effective leadership pipeline to ensure that leadership at the top is in place and to prepare for transitions.* A good measure of success is that 100 percent of all key retirement eligible positions have backups in place.

The key areas that organizations can address to help facilitate effective planning and successful transitions include:

- creating a positive management mindset
- looking for ways to retain key employees before and after retirement
- creating total rewards for employees to want to assist in transitions
- identifying recruiting requirements to address gaps that cannot be filled by internal promotions
- examining policies ensuring these support your transition
- creating roles for the retirees to fill, and mentor newly appointed successors

One of the key industry trends in the '90s was to flatten organizations and take layers out for a variety of reasons, including reducing costs, getting closer to the customer, and speeding up decision-making. As a result, the risks associated with moving high potentials into new roles for development increased significantly.

For example, in one restaurant company client a regional VP may have more than one hundred units with ten direct reports. In another restaurant company client, the regional VP may have fifty restaurants with seven direct reports. Take a guess which VP role would be more of a risk as you promote a direct report? We have eliminated in many cases the development jobs that in the past would serve as feeder roles into the key jobs, thus increasing the risks for development.

Executive coaching, when deployed against these best practices, serves as an enabler to achieve the objectives for smooth transitions and business sustainability. Using coaching to help create a culture of development for retention of key employees and helping in the mentoring and new leader assimilation processes is a significant help for companies facing the issue of the brain drain. Executive coaching with purposeful intent and directed at real business issues creates a much greater accountability and impact on the business than the traditional deployment of coaching for development.

WRIGHT

What is your executive coaching process? How does your framework help organizations address internal knowledge gaps?

A critical focus for dealing with top leadership and technical gaps that may exist is to develop a system for performance transformation. We call this our Performance Transformation System. The system applies to individual leaders, teams, and organizations. The system has a series of critical steps that are essential to success. Let me describe these steps:

The first step is to clearly describe where you are going or need to be as an organization. We help companies by assisting in developing the vision, mission, values, and strategies if these do not exist. After all, if you don't know where you are aiming and don't have clear plans in place, with measures of progress toward the goals, it is difficult to achieve success.

For example, we are working with a large consumer products organization. Their vision and direction were clear, but the leadership attributes and corporate culture changes required to implement a growth and expansion strategy were not clear. The organization had operated primarily in the Southeast and needed to expand to other parts of the country for sustained growth over the long-term. As a result, the culture needed to be adapted to ensure more diversity and openness to other approaches, methods of business, and styles of leadership. Operating a decentralized business was a core competency, but moving outside their comfort zone posed challenges on the senior leadership team. In addition, the leadership team was going to change with potentially three of seven top executives retiring in five years.

The second step is to outline where you need to excel in the individual leader, team, and organizational levels to achieve the direction you intend to go.

In other words, what competencies as individual leaders, leadership teams, and in the organization as a whole are critical to success? The answers to these questions are important to figure out what you have to develop for the future, and where leaders of the future need to excel in the new organization. We refer to these as competencies or those critical skills, abilities, knowledge, and attributes essential for success in the future.

Some examples may help to illustrate the essence of this step. With one client, the organization had enjoyed years of growth through record-breaking product development and outstanding pharmaceutical products. The organization was plateaued and the level of new products had slowed considerably. For leaders, one of the key competencies to be developed was to exhibit stronger entrepreneurial leadership that involved establishing a work environment of empowerment and performance. Some example leadership behaviors in that regard were:

- Fosters entrepreneurial spirit by encouraging initiative and calculated risk taking,
- Ensures individual and team objectives are linked with strategy,
- Sets challenging goals.

Working with another client, this organization was organized into operating units that were supported by functional departments such as legal, finance, HR, IT, and marketing. Over the years, strong internally focused specializations for the support departments and a lack of proactive support of the operating units developed. There was little teamwork and collaboration for the top team in the day-to-day operations of the business.

One of the key competencies required for the team to compete effectively in the future was increased collaboration and teamwork. As a result, the top leadership team had to develop competencies in the areas of effectively resolving conflicts, enhanced communications, improved team decision-making, and teamwork.

The last example I would like to mention is at the organization level, which is also critical to success. One of the clients we worked with was implementing a very aggressive growth strategy, which was fueling the support they enjoyed on Wall Street and subsequently their stock multiples. The analysts were valuing their stock at very high multiples based on the prospect of a very rapid growth expectation. Their core business was the identification and distribution of pharmaceutical products. As a result, this company needed to become very competent in product innovation and execution of growth plans. Both of these competencies are difficult to achieve without moving through the next steps of our process, as you will understand more as you read on about the next steps.

The third step is to assess the current competencies, whether that is at the individual leader, team, or organizational level. The methods and types of assessments vary by the level, but the foundation is to understand how you stack up to the required level of competency needed—what the strengths and weaknesses are. Our approach for leaders is to use a comprehensive assessment including 360-degree interviews and surveys, personality assessments, and self-reports.

We always recommend two comparison points for the measures. The first is on a relative basis within the measurement system you deploy. For example, if the measure is leadership competencies, and a one means in the bottom 10 percent of leaders and a five is in the top 10 percent of leaders, you can look at the averages to get a reading on relative strengths and weaknesses. That can be misleading and we use caution when only using this measure. If a leader scores competent or a three on the five-point scale, one may conclude the leader is fine, with little needed improvements. We like to add an external benchmark also, to compare the competencies to a best practice pool of international leaders. Adding this dimension to the evaluation brings out another level of comparison. In the example I just mentioned, comparing the averages of three to four on the five-point scale may be far different if the seventy-fifth percentile scores are all between four and five. That gap causes much more motivation for changes and improvements.

The other aspect to our consideration of where individuals, teams, and organizations stand on the key competencies is to ensure that the most important competencies for success are prioritized and known. After all, we want people to focus on the most important competencies, and not to waste their time and efforts on competencies that don't really matter.

The fourth step is to develop the action plans that address what you intend to develop, improve, or leverage.

In the leadership development arena, we see organizations take a wide range of actions from classes on leadership to actual job changes. We know from research and experience that learning leadership in the classroom has far less value than moving into positions and actually learning and applying leadership on the job. There are some very effective methods in between placing people in new roles and learning in a classroom. Action learning, where leaders work on real business issues at levels normally higher than their current roles (when organized and moderated) have very impressive results on leadership skills development. Also, 360-degree feedback and executive coaching have been shown to be more effective in developing leaders than just classroom learning.

The fifth step involves implementation of the plans. There are critical success factors to ensuring plans are implemented effectively, including documenting the goals, actions, timetables, creating measures to monitor progress, and having frequent and deep reviews of progress, and addressing shortfalls as needed. We are often helping organizations implement leadership development plans for succession planning purposes, and we specifically utilize 360-degree feedback, executive coaching, and action learning to develop leadership skills and performance.

The two specific instances where executive coaching for success is most helpful are in the development of high potentials to take leadership roles and in instances when a new leader is appointed.

For developing high potentials, the focus is on accelerating their development and exposure so that they can move into leadership roles when these become available. The coaching process is standardized and incorporates all of the elements outlined in the system so far, as well as the next two steps of the system.

For new leader assimilation coaching, there is a specific application designed to bring a newly appointed leader to 100 percent productivity in a shorter amount of time. By applying specific coaching toward the early problems, challenges, and issues encountered, along with a specific one-hundred-day assimilation plan for the business, the executive stands a greater chance to succeed. About 40 percent of newly appointed executives fail to meet the job standards in the time allotted. Using new leader assimilation coaching provides a number of benefits to the newly appointed leader, including insurance against failure.

The sixth step is to measure and track performance to goals set. For the executive leader, this can be done by measuring progress toward his or her goals, changes in leadership effectiveness or competencies, and changes in the tangible aspects of the business. Our typical measures include frequent progress checks with key stakeholders, mini-360 degree surveys of goal attainment, and change year over year in leadership competencies, along with changes in employee development and commitment.

The last step is to evaluate the complete process in the previous steps and make changes necessary for improvement in the next cycle or situation.

WRIGHT

Why do most organizations fail to produce the leaders required to meet the business's requirements?

BROOKMIRE

The most important processes for addressing the knowledge gap are effective succession planning and leadership development. There are many assumed truths about these processes that have become widely accepted and actually are no longer relevant or applicable. These assumed truths together end up producing processes that fail to deliver.

Some of the assumed truths include:

- HR owns succession planning;
- You can teach people to be leaders through training and development programs;
- Systems and processes are essential to success;
- Assessments made in the process are 100 percent accurate;
- Moving people to new jobs by itself will produce leaders (as opposed to having new leader assimilation).

Succession planning has been around for more than fifty years in one form or fashion. Today's approaches to succession planning are in many ways the same as in the past with the exception of more advanced technology tools to facilitate the process. Too often succession planning becomes an HR program and fails to actually develop leaders by not getting real action on leadership development beyond internal and external training and development programs.

- What succession planning is really good at is creating a process, identifying competencies, assessing potential, reporting results, and monitoring and reporting progress.
- Where succession-planning fails is the actual development of leadership in an effective and efficient manner.

That is where the process stops or the actions are too watered down for any real substantial development of leadership. Like any good process, while planning is key, execution and implementation are also essential to success, not just the evaluation and planning process

WRIGHT

How did you get started addressing the knowledge gap with organizations?

BROOKMIRE

I started very early in my career, both in graduate school and with my first job out of college. My degrees are in Industrial/Organizational Psychology and I am a licensed psychologist. I have been continually learning and expanding my knowledge, skills, and experience in the areas of organization effectiveness and leadership development.

Right from my PhD program, I went to work for General Motors in their corporate human resources department. My job was to assess talent and manage a process for succession planning for the most senior roles. My role was to ensure and assist with development of the high potential pool of leaders across the organization (5,500 at the time), which included the future top executives of the company. Back in the '80s and '90s, many vacancies were going to occur in large part due to retirement. If you recall, GM was steeped in tradition with joining the company and remaining there for your entire career. For example, when I was there after college, many of my peers had twenty-five years with the company.

My next role was with Frito Lay, and at the time I was there, we were the exporter of talent—primarily top leadership—into the broader Pepsico system. A large part of my job focus was on the identification, development, and exporting of talent from all functions of the company, but primarily in marketing, finance, and operations. Backfilling these key moves was critical to business continuity.

After that role I became the senior HR leader at a technology company that was growing in large part due to acquisitions. Like most technology companies in the '80s and '90s, we had our fair share of turnover at all levels. As the senior HR leader, my role was to provide a support function to the operating heads that created an effective talent management system.

The next role I filled was as senior HR leader at a rapidly growing financial services company. The company grew organically and through acquisitions. During my tenure, the company grew from $35 million to $400 million in about five years. The rapid growth created all types of strains on our talent to keep up with the needs of the business. In addition, we were losing key talent after acquiring their companies and in the business we were in—professional services—the core assets were only the people and customers, and no other real tangible assets. Every time a key employee voted with his or her feet and left the company, we had significant gaps of knowledge, experience, customer loyalty, and productivity to fill.

In our consulting business we have been helping clients in various stages of the product life cycle deal with succession planning and talent management. As an aside, we see real differences in the competencies required of leaders along the various stages of the product life cycle.

WRIGHT

Give me a quick overview of your company.

BROOKMIRE

I started our company with the client experience in mind. Our focus was on helping organizations achieve desired performance results and goals. We are senior leaders who have had successful corporate careers and for a variety of reasons have chosen to work as consultants helping many organizations realize their potential.

In essence, we help companies achieve measurable results by:

- Identifying leadership requirements from the company's strategy, culture, and environment,
- Comparing the current leaders to an international sample of best practices,
- Developing plans for performance improvements and leveraging strengths,
- Helping our clients implement their plans.

WRIGHT

You have been in business for seven years. What is the key to your long-term success?

BROOKMIRE

Our keys to success have been:

1. Our business is comprised of clients who ask us to do more and more work with them after our initial engagement.
2. Repeat business and long-term client relationships help us grow and succeed as a consulting business.
3. My belief is that if you do what you say you will do and more, produce high quality work, learn the client's business, and because you form deep relationships as a trusted advisor, you create a sustainable business.
4. Another key attribute for us is a practical approach to consulting—one where we care about what it is like to not only develop solutions, but implement them as well. Since all of us in the firm spent the majority of our working careers inside companies in key leadership roles, we know what clients go through to produce work and that addresses their needs.

About the Author

DAVID BROOKMIRE IS A SEASONED executive advisor and recognized authority on organization and leadership effectiveness. Working extensively with CEOs and senior leaders across the globe, David provides trusted advice and counsel, assisting these leaders in achieving their organizational goals and commitments. Specifically, he provides CPS clients with strategic direction and creative vision in the areas of business continuity, merger and acquisition success, improved leader and team performance, and HR effectiveness.

David's experience in business and consulting is extensive. His approach combines more than two decades of successful roles as a senior executive with global responsibilities and specific education in Industrial and Organizational Psychology to provide unique perspective to clients of all sizes and industries. David utilizes his expertise to develop, design, and implement innovative business and performance enhancement strategies and initiatives that help clients capitalize on business opportunities and overcome critical barriers to success. Representative clients include Kodak, Lucent, ADP, Flowers Foods, Platinum Equity, Darden Restaurants, Solvay, Randstadt, Georgia State University, Doosan, Arthritis Foundation, Pitney Bowes, Royal Bank of Scotland, and Merial.

Throughout his career, David's strategies have directly contributed to numerous measurable benefits on behalf of his clients, including executive leadership performance improvements, retaining highly valued at-risk executives, improved top-line growth, successful IPO, acquisitions, and divestitures, rapid and critical skill acquisition and retention, successful business strategy development and implementation, improved workforce productivity, M&A integration success, and creating winning teams and strong corporate cultures. Prior to founding CPS, David held several executive positions with well-recognized companies including Frito-Lay, General Motors, Digital Communications, and Profit Recovery Group. Among his corporate accomplishments, David has the distinction of managing global HR effectiveness, business strategy, and merger integration in his executive positions. He has also assisted foreign buyers from Japan and other countries successfully acquire businesses domestically. His understanding of globally applicable business best practices and international economics is truly a unique offering to his clients.

In addition to his client service career, David is a recognized speaker and expert in leadership development and business effectiveness. His national workshops include "Designing a High Quality M&A Process that Delivers" and "Managing and Leading High Impact Executive Coaching in Your Organization." His presentations on business strategy and human resource improvement have been presented to diverse audiences ranging from Wall Street analysts to corporate board members.

David earned a BA, MA, and PhD from the University of South Florida. He serves as a board member for Quality Care for Children and is active in his community.

DAVID BROOKMIRE

Corporate Performance Strategies, Inc.
1875 Old Alabama Road, Suite 520
Roswell, GA 30076
770.587.2265
info@cpstrat.com
www.cpstrat.com

David Brookmire

Chapter 7

Rudy Ruettiger

DAVID WRIGHT (WRIGHT)

Today we're talking with Rudy Ruettiger. Against all odds on a gridiron in South Bend, Indiana, Daniel Rudy Ruettiger in twenty-seven seconds carved his name into history books as perhaps the most famous graduate of the University of Notre Dame. The son of a old refinery worker and third of fourteen children who rose from valleys of discouragement and despair to the pinnacles of success, today is one of the most popular motivational speakers in the United States. It took years of fierce determination to overcome obstacles and criticisms, yet Rudy achieved his first dream: to attend Notre Dame and play football for the fighting Irish. As fans cheered, "Rudy! Rudy!" he sacked the quarterback in the last twenty-seven seconds of the only play in the only game of his football career. He is the only player in the school's history to be carried off the field on his teammate's shoulders. In 1993 Tristar Productions immortalized his life story with the blockbuster film *Rudy*, written and produced by Angelo Pizo and David Anspa. The award winning team that brought us the critically acclaimed *Hoosiers*, *Rudy* received "two thumbs up" from Siskel and Ebert and continues to inspire millions world-wide.

Rudy, thanks for being with us today!
Would you tell our readers what you are focusing on now as a career?

RUDY RUETTIGER (RUETTIGER)

There's a couple of things that I'm focusing on, health and nutrition. Number one, we feel that because of obesity and diabetes in children we should come up with better and healthier food and drink. We've developed a healthier drink for the kids, and also we're coming up with healthier food. Real food called Real Live Vegetables, all the veggies that you would want to eat in a day, and your fruits. Now you can get them in a powdered form that we've processed that we're very excited about. You can get them in a milk shake, and what it does is give you all your vitamins and fruits for the day. It's real fruit. That's what we're doing, we're very excited about that because we feel that no one else is going after what we are going after, so we decided to go after it. It's a tough market, but we believe that people will see the light and understand that their health is very valuable and nutrition is what we should pay attention to.

WRIGHT

In a recent conversation with you, we talked about some of the positive aspects of failure. You used the phrase, "The courage to fail." Would you tell us what you mean?

RUETTIGER

In anything that you do you are always wondering, "What if I don't make it?" Or what if this, or what if that? And what you have to look at is, don't look at the what if success doesn't happen—look at if it *does* happen, what are you going to do to correct it? So you need courage to fail. Don't worry about obstacles, because you can adjust to them as they show up because of your dream power and how you persevere through the tough times. You will find a way to get the job done. So my point is that most people worry about the failure, and if you just worry about the failure you'll never do it—so don't worry about the failure! Worry about what you have to do to get it done, and the victory will come. Also, through the failure you will learn from it, and then you can take it to the next level. That's what I meant by that.

WRIGHT

We also talked about rules and laws. You said something interesting, that people in business already know what to do, they should just *do it*. Would you elaborate for our readers?

RUETTIGER

Number one, a lot of people procrastinate. They procrastinate because they don't think the time is important right now, which it is. And when you "do it now" and you get it done, that when things take new life to it. Most people look for other answers to get it done, but if you just *get it done* you'll find out there's a lot of ways to get it done through ways that you never thought were there. But if you don't push through that criteria that I talk about, just get it done instead of looking why it won't get done, then you'll have a success again. So most people that I have looked at getting things done, they just get it done, they do what's important to get it done, and they do what's necessary to get it done, and they do whatever it takes to get it done! Those are very important elements for anyone who has a business or has a goal, they know it's easier to procrastinate and put it off. If you just to get it done, then the procrastination doesn't affect your thinking anymore. Procrastination comes from my feeling of, "What if I fail?" So don't worry about that, you can eliminate that goofy thought.

WRIGHT

We also talked a lot about our educational system and how attitude is so important. You remembered a teacher who said to her class, "No one makes an A in my class." What does this kind of statement do to our children in the classrooms of America?

RUETTIGER

Well, our teachers fail our kids, our kids don't fail—our teachers fail our kids. So what we have to look at is inspirational teachers, what I call "inspirational education." We can all learn from inspiration, and we learn differently through inspiration. But for kids who go there and say, "Okay, I got to get an A in this class," and the teacher comes in and says something like no one gets an A in my class—so why should I go to class if I can't get my goal? If you are going to stop me before I start, what's the use of even trying? That's what I'm talking about. I think if the teacher comes in and says, "Everybody gets an A in this class, and here's what you have to do to get it," this is all the criteria that's necessary for a successful student. Then they do the extra work, they do what's important, they do what it takes, and it all comes down to getting it done. But they're not inspired to get it done. Why would they go to work? Or why would they come to class? Or why would they pay attention? Hopefully they have a clear understanding of people who inspire you, or people who get it done. They have a wonderful network of people who can give them the right information, and I think that's what's important too—surround yourself with very knowledgeable important people who can get things done for you.

WRIGHT

We talked about passion and the importance of people discovering their passion. Do you think it's possible to develop passion in a person at the formal education level or in the training rooms of our corporations?

RUETTIGER

Oh, absolutely. Absolutely. Especially they are a part of a good team or a good family, if they are a part of something big. Most people want to be a part of something, and they get passion about that. And they get new dreams and new goals because of that. They get hope because of that! So my point is if I've got a teacher coming in and saying that no one gets an A in their class, it shuts down the creativeness and creative juices of the students, and the vision. In our corporations and in our schools today we have to apply an inspirational thought process to enable people to become passionate.

WRIGHT

In researching for this interview I've been reading and hearing a lot about "the Rudy Way" and "the Rudy Culture." Was is that?

RUETTIGER

The Rudy Way is "put no limitations on you," that's the Rudy Way! And sometimes you're going to go through the back door. It's like a little ten year old boy goes to football practice and he's clumsy and the coach sees he can't be one of us, and all of sudden he sees that he runs and he's fast—then the coach says that the boy is fast, but he's not coordinated yet, maybe I can get him into track and help his coordination. So he gives him a new goal, track, and he finds out he's good at track, and then he gets excited, then he finds out he can jump the long jump and he'd only gone out there because the coach directed him toward what he can do at that point. A lot of us are not ready to do what we want to do, so why can't somebody else say, "Why don't you do that first and then let's see what develops?" And that's what I'm talking about. If you recognize the positive in yourself and do what you can do right now, the other things happen to you. It just does. Not only did this little boy find out he could jump, but he is the champion jumper! And by the way this is a true story, it's not something made up. This coach who saw this little boy who was clumsy but directed him towards something that he thought he could do to achieve a victory. And that's what's important, get a victory! Win something! And you get confidence, I think that's what's important.

WRIGHT

What role to you think inspiration plays in our country today? And what role should it play?

RUETTIGER

First of all, there's a lot of doom and gloom out there, it's all we hear. But when you see people who inspire people, it changes your behavior and your attitude. If I go to work and listen to the information coming down the rail that "everything's bad," why do I want to go to work? It's kind of a gloom and doom day. But if I go to work knowing that things are going to get better if I just work a little harder, and if we do this a little differently, I have a different attitude and behavior. Now I approach my work, my company, my family, and everything. So inspiration does become a big asset, being inspired through music or a good story, being inspired through a good book or someone you can listen to who inspires you—I think that's the key, listening to good information! And even though that reality is out there, you can overcome adversity by handling it differently with a positive thought process and behavior.

WRIGHT

If, as we have discussed, failure is okay because we only learn from failure, what about the risks versus the safety net factor? Don't most of us want to play it safe?

RUETTIGER

Absolutely, it's a normal behavior. It really is a normal behavior for all people to play it safe. They like their comfort zone. Once they're in their comfort zone, it's where they stay. The entrepreneurs, the people who make it, are the ones who take that risk. In fact they create their own safety net. The only person who can be fired by anybody is *you* now, because you're the boss. You can fire yourself. Or, if you're going to work, the only person who can fire you is your boss—so why don't make yourself so valuable to your boss that he can't fire you? So there's all different kinds of ways of approaching it I guess and looking it, but you do learn from failure. You do learn from that type of struggle. But that doesn't say you're not qualified to do the work that you're intended to do. So don't get discouraged because something like that happens, just understand that it's a part of what I call the bridge that you build to your next dream or your next success.

WRIGHT

You have four books out now. Would you tell our readers why you wrote them, and are they helping to do what you intended them to do?

RUETTIGER

Well, Rudy's Style was written because I wanted to clearly tell people that if I made it, you can make it through hard work and perseverance and dream. And if you get through the struggle, and get realistic goals from that struggle, you will make it to where you want to go. It may not be what you thought, but it could be something better. For an example, my dream to play football at Notre Dame—I never dreamt of making a movie or being famous, I just wanted to walk through the tunnel. But because of that, look what happened because I didn't give up on that little goal. You don't know what's behind the next door. New opportunities happen when you pursue life this way.

WRIGHT

What are your plans for the future? How can we help you reach your goals?

RUETTIGER

My plans for my future are pretty simple. Do what I can do. Get around people who are important to point of what I call "insolence of where you want to go." That's how people help me get to where I have to go. Make sure you have the right product information to get your product to the next level. And I call it a grass root approach in life, and just tell people what you're doing and get people excited about what you're doing—that's how people help you! You asked me earlier what I am going to be doing with my health, and I said the nutrition aspect of it. You look at life like that, and that's what happens. I think you attract certain people, and you get good nutritionists around you, and you get good people who know the business around you. And then they direct you, and then you have to trust them to do what they know how to do. I don't think a lot of people let go enough to get things done, they want to take full control of everything and that's not good either. You got to let go a little and give it a chance. I watch a great coach, that's what he does—he gives a second chance to someone, and when that happens it happens for the right reason. Then he finds out there's a different talent in that kid, and it's like that at work too. You recognize a new talent in a secretary, and in order for that secretary to become the best that she can be, he sees something she can be good at and all of a sudden she's running the department she never dreamed that she could. These are examples that I see through life, but you have to be open to that. You have to be open to all that, you have to embrace that energy—you cannot control the energy, you have to allow energy to take care of itself, the positive energy. That's what happens, everybody I'm around that are very successful there are no rule changes—the rules are to be flexible, the rules are to allow people to be what they want to be and encourage people. Inspire people, set certain structure in the deal and you'll be surprised what happens.

WRIGHT

You know because of your celebrity you've appeared on a lot of different kinds of media like People Magazine, Sports Illustrated or U.S. Magazine,

Reader's Digest, Inside Sports, The 700 Club, the list goes on. NFL Films, CBS Good Morning, ABC Good Morning, NBC, Regis and Cathy Lee, Motel Williams, Entertainment Tonight—the list goes on! And that's because you're a celebrity, but you know people listen to you. You're a motivational speaker. How does it feel? And what do you learn when from speaking on the same platform as you have with President Bush or Barbara Bush or Joe Montana or Colon Powell or Zig Zigler—how does that feel and what do you learn?

RUETTIGER

We all learn from each other, that's number one, because we all have something different to offer. Different talents go to different levels, but people help those talents go to that level. Those people are always open to people like myself, and I'm always open to people like them. That's why lunars, accept that information and accept that inspiration, and when you go speak with these type of people you may learn something much differently from them than you thought you could learn because they're so open and approachable. It's been very, very exciting for me to be around these great people. I don't look at it as celebrity status, because no one knows what I look like, but they know what the movie stands for. Someone once told me, "You know, Rudy, I'd rather have your status in life, people know what you stand for. No one knows what I stand for, but I sing a lot of records. And how many more records can I do and how many more songs can I sing? But no one really knows what I stand for." That's how I want to leave this earth, by people saying, "Now he stood for this, and stood for that."

WRIGHT

You were inducted into the Speakers Hall of Fame, what's that?

RUETTIGER

I think it's just one of those things that people give you to recognize you for your hard work. I'm not sure why, but I'm not sure why I get anything! I'm just happy to get it, does that make sense?

WRIGHT

That makes sense to me! So, any final thoughts on how our readers can own more of the Rudy Style of living?

RUETTIGER

I think the Rudy Style is, number one, be open. Don't accept the way that people say you have to get there, accept the way you have to get there. And look at different ways of getting there, because there's always a way. If you want it bad enough, you have that "want to" attitude, you'll find a way. You will figure out the way. And sometimes the backdoor way is the way to get there. There's story upon story of how having that style, that improve style, makes you very creative and very successful.

WRIGHT

Well, I really appreciate all the time you've spent with me answering all these questions, Rudy. I always enjoy talking to you, you're such an inspiration to a lot of people. I just want to thank you for spending this time with me today!

RUETTIGER

Thank you very much. And like I say, it always starts with some dream— and it's always too soon to quit. That's how I live my life!

About the Author

Against all odds on a gridiron in South Bend, Indiana, Daniel Rudy Ruettiger in twenty-seven seconds carved his name into history books as perhaps the most famous graduate of the University of Notre Dame. The son of a old refinery worker and third of fourteen children who rose from valleys of discouragement and despair to the pinnacles of success, today is one of the most popular motivational speakers in the United States. It took years of fierce determination to overcome obstacles and criticisms, yet Rudy achieved his first dream: to attend Notre Dame and play football for the fighting Irish. As fans cheered, "Rudy! Rudy!" he sacked the quarterback in the last twenty-seven seconds of the only play in the only game of his football career. He is the only player in the school's history to be carried off the field on his teammate's shoulders. In 1993 Tristar Productions immortalized his life story with the blockbuster film *Rudy*, written and produced by Angelo Pizo and David Anspa. The award winning team that brought us the critically acclaimed *Hoosiers, Rudy* received "two thumbs up" from Siskel and Ebert and continues to inspire millions world-wide.

RUDY RUETTIGER
www.rudyinternational.com

Chapter 8

Tony Alessandra

THE INTERVIEW

DAVID WRIGHT (WRIGHT)

Today we're talking to Tony Alessandra. Tony, when we decided on the title of *Coaching for Success* for our latest project, you were one of the first people that we thought exemplified success. You've built a successful company by helping other companies achieve market dominance in their industries. Where did it all start and why did you choose your profession?

TONY ALESSANDRA (ALESSANDRA)

Well David it's hard to put a finger on where it started. If you really want to know in my opinion were my attitude, and aptitude almost, for success started was when I was a little kid, and as strange as this may sound, I grew up in the projects of New York City, right in Manhattan, in the Chelsea section of New York City and my father was a New York City cab driver. We lived in the projects which is the lower income area of the city, there were several of these areas, and one day I was down in the playground of the projects, which is really four large high rise buildings, all apartments, small apartments, and in the middle of these four buildings was a little playground, and some kid, older and bigger than me, he beat me up, that was my first fight. So I went upstairs, I think we lived on the 6th floor, I went upstairs crying, my father happened to be home and asked me what happened, and I really believe that this was a turning point in my life, one of the big turning points. He said to go back down and fight that kid again, that I'm living in New York City and if kids really feel that they can beat me up, they're going to bully me and it won't be safe for me. I said no, no, no, I was crying and I was afraid and are you ready for this? He took off his belt and he said, you're either going down and fighting that kid again or you're going to face the belt, and I knew the belt, so I said, alright I'm going back down and with that motivation, after just being beaten up by this kid, I went back down and I beat him up.

Now within a day one of his friends comes by and challenges to fight me, and I say this is only my second real fight, I fight this kid, again knowing what happened with that other kid, and I beat him up and what it did is it set years and years an attitude and a way I carried myself. I truly as a kid all the way through high school never lost, other than that very, very first time in the projects, never lost a one to one fight, and I carried a reputation. It's almost like the gunslingers in the Wild West, you know the fastest gun, kids would come from other neighborhoods to fight me. My cousin, when we finally moved to Brooklyn, New York, my cousin would bring kids home from his school, I was in a catholic school, he was in a public grammar school, he would bring kids home to fight me, you know because he was proud of me, but he'd bring these kids home and I created a reputation and it allowed me to carry myself in a way, a very successful way. So that was sort of my first start and it prompted kids not to put peer pressure on me to do things that they may have tried to get or force other kids to do, they kind of stayed away because of that.

When I went through school I actually was quite a good student, you know I got very good grades in school, I was sort of a trouble maker and got very mischievous in school and sort of a wise guy. Not that I went out looking for fights or anything like that, but I was sort of like a class clown, so I'd get in a lot of trouble with my teachers but I always got good grades, so even though it irritated them and I got detention every so often, they sort of gave me a little bit of slack because I did well in school, and that was another thing that kind of led to this concept of success. So it was the street fighting, it was my grades, then came sports and I found that I had sort of a natural aptitude towards sports, I excelled in baseball, I excelled in football, I never wrestled competitively in my life until I went to college. In college they never had an inter collegiate wrestling team, I went to the University of Notre Dame, and they didn't have an inter collegiate, but they had a intra collegiate, or intra mural wrestling, and it was pretty unbelievable, it was all classes, you know it wasn't all like freshman against freshman, it was freshman, sophomores, juniors and seniors, anybody as long as you were within a particular weight range and I decided, somebody kind of pushed me to do it because he had heard my stories about street fighting. So I entered the tournament and won a gold medal in my weight category, even though I had never wrestled before. And it just kept on, the dominoes kept falling that way, one success after another, after another.

I graduated Notre Dame, I went to grad school at the University of Connecticut and when I was there and graduated with an MBA I decided to take on a teaching position and after 3 years as a college teacher, I taught 2 years at Susquehanna University and 1 year at Cal State Fullerton. I decided that I wanted to make teaching a profession, so I enrolled in a Doctoral program for PhD in Marketing in Business at Georgia State University, and here really is a major turning point because one of the senior professors on the senior faculty at Georgia State University and in the Department of Marketing was a gentleman named Dr. David Schwartz. Dr. David Schwartz it so happened was the author of a book, one of the three books that I feel had an enormous impact on my life, the three books were; 30 Days to a More Powerful Vocabulary, because I really didn't have a good vocabulary, so that really jumped up my vocabulary and my articulation skills. The second book was Psycho Cybernetics by Maxwell Malts, really the mechanics of the mind, but the third book was called The Magic of Thinking Big, and lo and behold the author was Dr. David Schwartz.

So when I went to Georgia State University he became my Doctoral Dissertation Chairman and it so happens he was also a motivational speaker and that was sort of my impetus, my role model to actually enter the field of professional speaking. While I was a doctoral student from 1973 to 1976, in 1974 when I finally got all my course work out of the way and now was working on my oral exams and my dissertation is actually when I started doing outside consulting and training and speaking and it was because of Dr. David Schwartz, him being that role model. I taught--I got my doctorate in the Spring of '76, I taught for another two and a half years at the University of San Diego, that's what brought me out to California, but in December of

'78 I left teaching to go into speaking full time and although I was a good speaker, you know a solid speaker, from the time I started in the Fall of '74 I was doing it part time the Fall of '74 until I went full time in January of 1979. I was a good speaker and I continued to be a good speaker until the winter of 1981 and this was another major turning point in my success, there was gentleman named Bill Gove. Bill Gove was the first President of the National Speaker's Association and I did a one-on--one weekend coaching, speaker/coaching session with him for an entire weekend and it was then that he pulled me to the side and said, Tony when you are not trying to speak you are this playful, mischievous New York City Italian personality, but when you go to speak that prophesorial style comes to the forefront and he said, it's not working for you. He said, you're trying to do a style that isn't your natural style, he said, what you need to do is let more of that playful New York City Italian style come to the forefront of speaking and I got to tell you it was the major turning point in my career. Once I went that direction I went from good to very good and in fact that was in the Winter, like February of 1981, by the Summer of 1985 I was inducted into the Speaker's Hall of Fame, that's how big a turn around it was in my career.

So those were really, I think, some of the success forks, forks in the road, where if I went one way or the other way that sort of got me to where I'm at and got me into the profession of professional speaking.

WRIGHT

It's kind of strange, back in the early '70's, '73 Paul Myer introduced me to two of the three books that you mentioned which had an impact on me and my favorite speaker of all time was Bill Gove.

ALESSANDRA

And he really was good wasn't he? I likened Bill Gove to the George Burns of public speaking, he had that style and it looked like it was so easy to do, but it wasn't. He was so good, he was a master of his craft and we really miss him.

WRIGHT

Absolutely, I talked to him just months before he died. I tried to get him to do a coaching session, he wouldn't, and he said he didn't leave his house anymore. What a great speaker.

So it's been my experience that people must get excited to really achieve their goals and their dreams, you've been one of the most successful speakers in America for years, how did you learn to get people to listen and to create excitement in them?

ALESSANDRA

Well I think there is at least a couple of things here and there, might be more, but one is that no matter how important and how practical the message might be, if it's delivered in a dry way, you're not going to get people to listen to it. So you have to make education also entertaining, and you know that turning point with Gove, where I had more of that New York Italian and also the humor, I'm a storyteller and I knew that from the time I was a kid because I used to--when I was kid in high school, and especially in college I would tell stories about things that happened to me that would have groups of people, I'd have their rapped attention and I should have realized that I was a natural, gifted storyteller, and it wasn't just telling the story but was telling it in a compelling and a funny way, and I brought that to the platform and once I brought it to the platform you really get people's attention. They love to listen to stories, especially stories that leave them with a learning point, so that's the first thing.

Another way to get people to listen and create excitement is to bring it into their world, and what I do is before I give a speech I do a lot of information gathering and research with either the executive and the meeting planner and possibly even call up some of the attendees and ask will this fly, is it relevant, am I using the right language, do you use different language? So I try to make it real for them. Let me give you a good case in point; this coming summer, July of 2008 I'm giving a series of three speeches for a group called the Pampered Chef, the Pampered Chef--believe it or not I actually just realized this last night, they're owned at least partially, maybe totally by Warren Buffet. So it was started by a woman named Doris Christopher, and back in 1995 they brought me in the first time to give a speech and it went well enough that they brought me back again 1998. So I did two talks for them. Now 10 years passed and they're looking for another speaker and they ask all of their highest executives who would you like to bring back in all the years you've been associated with the Pampered Chef and I'm just telling you what they told me, my name kept coming up over and over again, so they brought me back, I'm going back July of this year. And I said, okay now that I'm coming back I want to do two things. Give me the names of 5 people who were in my session in 1998 and I want to ask them two questions; what was it that I did in 1998 or how did my talk in 1998 impact their career and their success? And number two, now that I'm coming back 10 years later and they're even higher up in the organization and they have many of their people coming to this meeting, what would they like their people to hear from me? So I called each of those 5 people, they gave me the answers to those questions, I told them to make sure they come up to me at the various sessions, because I'm doing 3 separate talks.

At each of these sessions there are like 4,000 people, so they can't fit them all in at one time, and then Pampered Chef is high end kitchen equipment and utensils, everything from cookware to knives, to baking equipment to little gadgets and they do home shows. So what I did is I said, could you set me up to go to one of the shows so that I can see what's changed, what's new? Again how it's done, how they interact with the people, with the women who are there. So I went to one last night, so that's how I--I don't do this for every speech not to this depth, but because this is such a good client and I'm back for the third time and I'm doing 3 programs to thousands of people I wanted to go the extra mile for them, and I have to tell you it really does make a difference because when I go in there I can tell stories and give examples that these women are going to be sitting back and saying, whoa this guy really knows what we do, and once they understand that I know what they do and I've gone the extra mile to learn what they do, they're going to take my message much more seriously.

So that's how I get people to listen, I tailor the message to them by doing my homework and I tell stories and make it entertaining but in that entertainment I describe it as making sure that they take their medicine, which is a key concept, but the medicine is wrapped in candy. So that's the humor, but it's there. So that's what I do.

WRIGHT

You're the founding partner of the Platinum Group that's based on the platinum rule, I know the golden rule but can you tell us what is the platinum rule?

ALESSANDRA

Well before I tell you what the platinum rule is let me just clarify something, it's called PlatinumRuleGroup.com, I'm the founding partner of Platinum Rule Group.com. The platinum rule is sort of a little twist to the golden rule. Everybody knows the golden rule which is do unto others as you would have them do unto you, and I have to tell you I believe in that rule, and I practice that rule, and I follow that rule and I follow that rule 110% when it comes to values, ethics, honestly, consideration, I've got to tell you there's no better rule to live by. However when it comes to one-to-one communication, whether it is simple conversation with family and friends, whether it is a sales situation, customer service, whether it's managing, motivating, counseling, coaching employees, the golden rule itself can back fire and the reason is that maybe not everybody wants to be treated the same way as you do and in this world today of every increasing diversity, and when I say diversity I'm talking about gender diversity, male/female, I'm talking about generational diversity, Gen X, Gen Y, Baby Boomers. I'm talking about personality diversity, outgoing, shy, right brained, left brained I'm talking about ethic diversity, everything from Italians, and Germans, and Americans, and I can go on and on, religious diversity, racial diversity, there's a lot of diversity today, and the golden rule, you know treating people the way you want to, treating people from your point of view just doesn't cut it.

So that's where the platinum rule came into being, the platinum rule and I have the federal trade mark of the platinum rule, is do unto others as they would have you do unto them. In other words treat people the way that they want and need to be treated. It's no different than that age old saying when in Rome do as the Romans, and I've got to tell you I learned that first hand when I moved from New York, New Jersey to Southern California. When I moved here to Southern California and you know that it's a very different regional culture isn't it, well when I moved to San Diego I treated people in San Diego according to the golden rule, I treated them the way I wanted to be treated. I treated them as if they were New Yorkers. Well I got to tell you it backfired, I came on too strong, too fast, too aggressive, too impatient, and even when I asked people to do things, that under any other circumstances they would have willingly done, they dug in their heels, they stonewalled and it wasn't because of what I was asking that prompted them to do that, it was because of how, it was my approach, I simply rubbed them the wrong way. So that's what the platinum rule is about; the platinum rule is about a concept called adaptability, adaptability is your ability to change your approach or to change your strategy, or the situation, or the person you're dealing with. That's what the platinum rule is about.

WRIGHT

So if we're determined to use the platinum rule, can we actually discover what makes people tick, I mean their strengths and weaknesses, their likes and dislikes?

ALESSANDRA

Absolutely, in fact I've spent the last 35 plus years, since I was in my doctoral program at Georgia State doing research, writing, speaking on the subject of the platinum rule, and if you go to platinumrule.com or even platinumrulegroup.com, there are two different sites, or even Alessandra.com, any of those sites you will see my lifetime of work in this field. The platinum rule is based on a behavioral style, four style model, not unlike other models like DISC, or Social Styles, or True Colors, it basically says that people have a dominant pattern of behavior, it's not their only pattern but it's a dominant pattern of either being a director, a thinker, a relater, or a socializer, and if you really keep your eyes and ears open and watch what people do, and listen to what people say, and how they say it, in other words their verbal, vocal, and visual behaviors, they will actually tell you how to treat them.

What I teach people to do is to be able to pick up these signals, these signs, these cues, quickly and effectively. Make two simple decisions; is the person coming across right here and now as more open or guarded? And is the person coming across, right here and now, more direct or indirect? When you can make those two decisions it will tell you how to vary your pace and priority, should you go faster or slower, should you focus primarily on the relationship or the task and that's--I'm simplifying it here for us, but that's the model and it truly is a model that people get the absolute ah-ha. In fact earlier I was telling you about my upcoming programs this summer for the Pampered Chef, well in 1995, 1998, and again in 2008, I'm giving the exact same speech, now there are changes, there's new examples and stories, new slides, but it's all on the platinum rule and they have incorporated this and many of the companies that I speak for incorporate this philosophy of the platinum rule. Now they may not use my terminology, they may not use director, thinker, relater, socializer, they may use driver, expresser, analytical, amiable, or DISC or whatever they use, they may use colors or animals, whatever, the basic concept is people are different and if you can really understand where they're coming from, right here and now, you can actually get on their wave length.

Let me just give you one final example here, my dominant pattern is that of the director, bottom line, no nonsense, fast paced, a little bit more guarded, only in the use of my time, I don't like people to waste my time, I've got a lot to do, but from being Italian I'm generally open in terms of telling people about what I feel and think. But generally in a business setting I am a director, a driver, a dominant, bottom line, no-nonsense, Donald Trump type of guy, so when somebody calls me, let's take one person in particular, my partner in Platinum Rule Group, his name is Scott Zimmerman. When Scott calls me--I can see on my caller ID it's Scott and it really depends on what's going on with me right then and there when he calls, I may answer the phone, yea what do you want? Now he knows I'm in my director mode, he's really good at this, he knows I'm in my director mode and he says Tony, one thing, no he doesn't even say, Tony hi how are you, he gets right to the point in terms of task and speed, Tony one thing and it's going to make you money. It's a quick call and he hangs up.

Another time he might call, I know it's him and I'm in a little bit different mood, I don't have time pressures, I'm not working on a deadline, I'm feeling pretty good, I'm caught up, I don't have to leave the next day for a speech, so I might answer it, Tony's Pizzeria what kind of toppings do you want? Then he says, oh give me some anchovies and some mushrooms, then we laugh and he says, what's going on over there? So you see it's a little bit more upfront schmoozing before we get down to the reason he calls. So that's what this whole concept is about. I mean we can get into things like left brain, right brain, outgoing, shy, time disciplines, time flexible, all these things play into whether somebody is more direct or indirect, or more guarded or open, and once you understand where somebody's coming across at that particular period in time, you know, or what the person's dominant style is, you know what makes them tick, their strengths, their weaknesses, their likes and dislikes.

WRIGHT

Let's get back to helping big companies build market dominance; do you start at the top with management or with company employees to implement successful strategies?

ALESSANDRA

Well if it's at all in your power you always want to start at the top, because if you don't start at the top and you start at the bottom the bottom people are going to be looking at the top people, and if the top people are not behaving in the way you're asking the bottom people to behave, the employees to behave, they're going to say, hey this is not supported by upper management, this is a do as I say, not as I do. You've got to get upper management involved and it's got to be pushed down from the top and the top has to model what it is you're asking the employees to do.

WRIGHT

So what happens when good employees want to hang on to the strategies of the past and resist change, is it best to terminate them and move on or do you really believe we can modify their behavior over time?

ALESSANDRA

I am a trainer and as a result I believe you can modify behavior, but let's talk about that because there's two questions here, what about people that want to hang on to the strategies of the past? What you need to do is make sure that when you're asking people to adapt to change, a lot of people simply focus on what you're asking them to change, and they make such a big deal about it. What you need to do when you're introducing change, you need to explain not only what's changing, but how many things are staying the same. In any organization, in any family, in any environment, when you're creating change, probably 80 to 95% of what they're doing stays the same. I mean you're only asking them to change a fraction of the overall picture. And I think when people see that that can feel a little more comfortable and then you need to explain why the change is important, what's in it for them, what are they getting out of it, and then you have to ask them to make that change over a period of time. If people can't or won't modify their behavior, do you terminate them, or do you change.

Remember back to that absolutely groundbreaking book called the One Minute Manager, remember that book? It said, hey you set a goal and when people are moving toward the goal you reward them and when they don't move toward the goal, what they said was basically reprimand, however what I really believe that the purpose was is, when you set goals or behaviors that you want employees, or even, children, let's say, or students, I mean this applies to anybody, when you want them to change behavior, when they're moving in the right direction, at the right speed, at the right pace, toward the change you reward them, you reinforce, you coach, you give them pats on the back so they keep going in the right direction. You know all of us in the training business know this old saying, inspect what you expect, so you want to make sure when you're asking for things to change, or you're asking for a particular type of behavior that people know you're going to look for it, you're going to inspect it, and then when they're moving in the right direction at the right speed, you reward them, and when they're not, at least the first time, you retrain, maybe the second time, you retrain. Now there comes a point where if retraining is not working, you've really got to explore do I terminate, because maybe the person just can't do it or isn't getting it, or doesn't want to do it. So that's my answer to that.

WRIGHT

As President of AssessmentBusinessCenter.com you offer 360 degree assessments, what is that and how does it help people?

ALESSANDRA

Well there are a lot of what they call online assessments, and online assessments measure people's behavior. Now people's behavior can be their leadership style, their selling style, their behavioral style, their emotional intelligence. You've seen all these different things, where people go online, they answer questions, and we call it an assessment and not a test, because a test is--in people's minds a test connotes there are right and wrong answers, where an assessment simply is measuring where a person is, so at my site, which is called assessmentbusinesscenter.com I have probably 25 different assessments that measure everything from diversity and cultural awareness, to emotional intelligence. Various fore style models like the Platinum Rule, True Colors, DISC, Social Styles, leadership, sales, it just goes on and on. What we try to do, we ideally, in some of these we do pre-tests and post tests, so for instance, let's take either leadership or sales, because those are two very interesting ones. We have somebody take the leadership or sales assessment and it typically is what they call a 360 or multi radar assessment, so the person, the end user, or the subject, whatever we want to call them, they take the assessment in terms of how they think they're performing on all these different categories, in terms of whether it's selling skills or leadership skills, Then we ask them to send the same set of questions to representative groups of people. So let's say for leadership we would have them send it to their manager, the person they report to, to their peers that they work with but don't have any control over and to their direct reports, so they get this--that's what they call the 360 review, and then we start seeing, not individual answers, but a composite of answers of how these various groups of people actually see us performing that behavior.

So we see how we saw our behavior and then look at how others see our behavior, and see if it's better or worse. We do the same thing with sales, but with sales we don't do quite the same thing. For a salesperson, a salesperson answers the questions on how they do on the various aspects of selling and then asks their sales managers, their fellow sales people and the key group; their customers or clients. Then we potentially put the manager/leaders, or the sales people, or whatever, we put them through a training program, whether it is a seminar run by somebody like me, a live program, or whether it is a self study program where they're going through an online, e-learning program, or an audio video learning program, whatever it is, they go through this program and we give them probably at least 30 days after they're finished with the program, in the field the rule of thumb is somewhere probably between 30 and 90 days after the program to implement some of these newly learned skills and behaviors. Then we have them go back again, answer the questions themselves, how they think they're performing now, and then go back to that same group of people and ask them, rate me now, and now we see, hopefully, improvement as a result of the training program, the live program, or the self study program, and that tells us how our training and learning is impacting, hopefully positively impacting behavior, but that's what we do with these assessments.

I build assessments, these are not just my assessments, I have an assessment platform, a technology platform that I developed for me back in 1996 for my Platinum Rule assessment, because that's when my Platinum Rule came out, and I was hoping to sell more books, but then all the sudden people started coming to me, Brian Tracy, Ken Blanchard, The University of Phoenix, HRD Press, and it goes on and on, people coming to me saying, hey could you put my assessment on your platform because your platform is so technologically advanced, and that's what I do and actually it's now become a bigger business for me, in terms of revenue, than my speaking business.

WRIGHT

Tony it seems as if you're not only a speaker but you've got these other businesses here, the assessment in doing other business, that seems like leading edge to me.

ALESSANDRA

It is and again, let me just go back David--I have a strong education background, I have a PhD in Marketing I was a college prof. for eight and half years, and when I went into professional speaking one of my biggest frustrations was, how can I change people's behavior in a one hour speech? I can motivate them, I can give them a tip here or there, but when I leave, if you go to education theory and brain theory, within two weeks they've lost probably at least 75% of what I've told them. So I've always been looking for ways to make education and learning and training stick, and that's why I formed the Platinum Rule Group, that's why I got into Assessment Business Center, I even became chairman of a company called BrainX.com, and it is a cutting edge e-learning technology that doesn't just take people through e-learning, self paced e-learning, it creates learning mastery and what that is, is the ability to remember, recall, and effectively use the material that you've learned. A lot of e-learning programs simply have people go through, and as long as they can pass a test at the end they're happy, but a week or two later could they pass that test again, but with BrainX they would because the technology is cutting edge and I'm always looking for things like that, like Platinum Rule Group, like Assessment Business Center, like BrainX.com.

I even got involved in a technology--are you familiar with the terminology CRM, customer retention management? It's database like ACT and Goldmine, those kinds of programs, those kinds of programs Outlook, where you can take all your customers and clients and put them in a database so that you can keep in touch with them, well the problem with that is that--you know you can have a thousand people in your database and all the sudden you're kind of going through your database, by accident you see a name and you say, oh my God David Wright, Insight Publishing, oh geez I haven't, I forgot--I haven't contacted him in a year, I should have stayed in touch with him. Well we created this new system, this new software called Cyrano, and it's a play off the concept or the play, the book Cyrano De Bergerac, and the site is called TheCyranoGroup.com and our software is automated software. So let's say that after today David I put you in my database and I ask you a couple questions; David if I were to stay in touch with you, what are some of the things you would like me to send you information about? Leadership, sales, time management, self development, whatever? Either I can ask you 4 or 5 quick questions or I can say, would you mind if I sent you a link, would you mind simply answering these 4 or 5 questions, and what it does is it puts you in my database, not just as a name, but now I know some things about you, and every time I send you stuff, by the way I'm only send you stuff that you clicked off about, and every time you get an email from me, at the bottoms, you know how sometimes it says if you don't want to hear from me anymore you can unsubscribe, but it also says if you would like to update your preferences click here, and you can always update what you're interests, your goals whatever, and the system will automatically send things to you, and I am constantly putting in articles and stories or whatever from every source imaginable, all of my colleagues in the National Speakers Association.

I mean thousands of articles are going into my system and then we click off what the article is about. Now if that matches what you were interested in, it will send you, eventually, it will send that article and I can send the article to you based on your style; are you a director, relater, thinker, socializer? It will tailor the intro to you about this article, and every day that my system automatically sends things to people, including happy birthdays, happy anniversary, happy anniversary of the first day we did business together, you name it, it will send me an email right after it sends out all the emails for the day, and it will tell me everybody they sent emails to and what it sent so that I can't be blind sided by you calling me 3 or 4 months from now saying, hey Tony thank you for that article, it was great. And I say, article what article? You know it tells me. I might say, David, yea I know you like golf and I came across that article and I knew you would like it. In fact if I come across an article, let's say a really creative article, let's say a really creative article on retirement or on sports or whatever and I scan it in to the Cyrano system and I click on retirement, or golf, or football, or whatever and I say find me all the people who are interested in that, my system will pull up all the names and I can then say send this article out to them, and it will send it out to everybody.

WRIGHT

Sounds like to me that's a practical application of the Platinum Group.

ALESSANDRA

Exactly, exactly, in fact the Platinum Rule Group, my partner Scott Zimmerman, he's my partner in the Cyrano Group and he's the guy who really developed this whole system, so I'm always--David, I'm always looking for ways that I can take what I teach and preach, put it into a practical, successful, cutting edge system and that's where PlatinumRuleGroup.com, AssessmentBusinessCenter.com, BrainX.com, TheCyranoGroup.com, that's where all that comes into play. I'm always looking for ways that I can deliver learning in a digital format that's cutting edge.

WRIGHT

On another subject, business owners tell me that customer loyalty is a major problem for them, they site everything from the changing attitudes of their customers to the World Wide Internet; how do you teach companies to retain their customers and build loyalty?

ALESSANDRA

What I teach people to do is to start this whole process of customer loyalty and customer retention in the prospecting stage, whether they are doing outbound prospecting, cold call prospecting, or whether they are getting their prospects from referrals, that what they need to do is profile their top 20%, their most profitable, most loyal customers and then start looking and searching and seeking referrals of prospects that fit the profile of their top 20%, that's the first step. Then I tell them, in the actual face to face selling process, to make sure that they are selling the right solutions to the customer's needs. Then I tell them, when it comes to the after sale service to make sure that they stay in touch with their customers so that we are constantly exceeding the customer's expectations, that we are creating as many moments of magic as possible for those customers, "wow" experiences, and to ultimately to develop deeper businesses and in some situations personal relationships with our customers so that we can convert them from a repeat customer to an apostle. An apostle is a raving fan, a business advocate, someone who is out there in the marketplace preaching the gospel for us, somebody who is giving us good word of mouth, somebody who is sending referrals to us. We don't even have to ask for them. That's the ultimate of customer loyalty.

So I teach people 4 sets of skills, marketing skills so that they can do appropriate prospecting and targeting, and niche marketing. Selling skills so that they match solutions to real customer needs, service skills so that they're constantly identifying, managing and monitoring customer experiencing so that we can exceed their expectations and then relationship skills so that we can convert our customers into apostles.

WRIGHT

You've written about creating value for customers and creating emotional attachments with them, can you tell our readers some examples of how that might happen?

ALESSANDRA

Well the key thing in creating value is making sure that during the information gathering stages of a sales process, we truly find out what the customer values, what's important to them, where does it hurt, where is the pain, and even asking questions like, if we are to sit down 3 or 6 months from now, after you start doing business for me, and as we're sitting here, reflecting back on the last 3, 6, 12 months, you're telling me, Tony doing business with you was an incredible positive decision. David what had to happen over those 3, 6, or 12 months to prompt you to say that to me, that doing business with you was a great business decision? And what you'll tell me is you're success criteria, what you'll tell me are your expectations, what you'll tell me is how you are determining the success of our relationship, you're telling me how I created value for you with my solutions, so that's one way.

Now creating emotional attachments is what I mentioned is converting repeat customers into apostles, and I've got to tell you, 80 to 100% of what we do to create emotional attachments has to do with our communication, our quantity and our quality of communication, and David I'm telling you that's one of the reasons we created The Cyrano Software at TheCyranoGroup.com was that we would have the right quantity and quality of communications, the messages are targeted specifically to the individual and their likes, dislikes, needs, goals, etc., even to the products that they purchase.

WRIGHT

You know I have been in the sales industry, well sales in a lot of industries for over 50 years, and I read a lot but I don't think I've ever come across what you are talking about which is collaborative selling, could you tell us what that is?

ALESSANDRA

Well collaborative selling is moving away from the more traditional approach where it's telling, selling, persuading, and I've got to tell you that's where I cut my teeth when I first learned how to sell, I mean I sold door to door, I learned how to use all the tricks and techniques, the psychology, the closing techniques, the overcoming objections skills, and what it did is it simply taught me how to make sales, not how to make customers. And collaborative selling sort of turns that on it's head, and what I did in the early '70's when I was a college professor, I really had the good fortune when I was a college prof., to be able to get any sales books ever written for free, and I got hundreds, and I truly mean hundreds of books and I poured through them looking for a better approach to selling and quite frankly it was rare that I found a tip or technique, or skill here or there. I really had to go outside of the sales literature into management, into coaching and counseling, into psychology and psychiatry and pull ideas out of there and the whole concept of collaborative selling was that, hey it's not me there selling your--it's us helping each other discover and solve your problems, so it relied on, instead of persuasive skills, it relied on questioning and listening skills, it required exploring the customer's needs and then when it came to-- and here's the key of collaborative; when it came to presenting a solution what was always taught, when we came up with a solution, the salesperson presented the solution, and even if it was the best solution it was the salesperson telling the customer, collaborative selling customer basically says, hey we're talking together, we're sharing ideas about what you're problems and needs are, what your goals and missed opportunities might be, and now when it gets into looking for potential solutions let's talk about the options, let's talk about the various things you can do, let's talk about the tradeoffs.

If you can do this or that, and what I want to do as we are collaborating I want you, Mr. Customer to basically tell me, I like that, I don't like that, this would work, this won't work, I like this better than that, I don't want that even though it's a good solution because the cost is beyond what I can do and basically you are helping me build the solution, whenever that's appropriate, by the way it's not appropriate in every sales situation with every product, but in many situations, if I can talk about options and trade-offs with the customer, and the customer helps me through this collaboration process build the solution, it's very difficult for a customer to say no to a solution that they helped build. That's what collaborative selling is all about.

WRIGHT

You know I have quoted you many times because I've read and listened to a lot of things that you've said and done, but one of the most insightful statements I've heard you say to date is, that people don't buy because they're made to understand, they buy because they feel understood. Can you explain what you mean and how I can best help people to feel understood?

ALESSANDRA

Absolutely, no question about it, you know one of the things we've done in collaborative selling, which was originally called Non-Manipulative selling, that was my very first book back in 1979. We had guiding principles and guiding principles were a prescription, before diagnosis was malpractice. People don't buy because they're made to understand, they buy because they're understood, the sale begins when the customer says, yes. Those kinds of guiding principles, but this one is a very interesting one in that it gets back to the crux of collaborative selling, and that is we're not selling, we're helping, we're not telling, we're asking, and people don't buy because they're made to understand all the features and benefits of your product, they buy because they feel that you understand them and their needs and that you're tailoring the solutions to those very specific needs. So it gets beyond the telling and selling to problem finding, problem solving, asking, listening, it's a whole different mentality. It's almost a play off of that other quote, it's not my quote, but people don't care how much you know until they know how much you care. It's a play off of that.

WRIGHT

Finally, Tony what's in store for you in the immediate future? Do you have any new projects? Do you have any more mountains to climb?

ALESSANDRA

Well I'm continuing David to go down this path of the internet, technology, digital delivery of material as opposed to having to ship things to people, again cutting edge learning skills. In fact a new project that I didn't even mention to you is called JITSS, Just In Time Sales Solutions and what I'm doing is I'm teaming up with an award winning film maker and what we're doing is we're creating 5 minute or less, bite size sales scenarios, we're putting together about 500 of them on very specific sales issues. For instance; how do I deal with the issue of a customer saying my price is too high or I want to think about it? Very, very precise, specific sales problems and here's what we're doing, we are filming it. I'm on screen for less than a minute setting the scenario about, how do you do a proposal, my price is too high, how do you ask an open ended question, what's the funnel technique? I'm only on screen describing less than a minute what it is and then you go into an approximate 4 minute actor role play where the actors, both as sales people and customers, the actors actually show you exactly how to do what it is I'm telling you. So you're not reading something, you're not listening to something, you're not watching me tell you how to do it, you are actually watching it done, you're seeing it role modeled the way it should be done in 5 minutes or less.

Then what we're doing is we are putting it into a database so that you can search for it and then click on it and boom there you have that 5 minute or less role model of a just in time sales solution to your problem and then I'm going even further with my assessments, adding more assessments, and the software that we're doing with this, the CRM, TheCyranoGroup.com, I'm doing all those things and trying to do less speaking. I'm trying to reach more people through the internet and the digital medium that I could in a year than I could in a lifetime giving live speeches.

WRIGHT

Well what a great conversation Tony, I have followed your work for years and I really do appreciate you taking all this time with me today to answer these questions, I have learned a lot and I am sure that our readers will.

ALESSANDRA

Well I really appreciate you thinking of me and including me in this project David and if another project comes up in the future where you think I can provide some benefit, you give me a holler, I'm here.

About the Author

Dr. Tony Alessandra has a street-wise, college-smart perspective on business, having been raised in the housing projects of NYC to eventually realizing success as a graduate professor of marketing, entrepreneur, business author, and hall-of-fame keynote speaker. He earned a BBA from the University of Notre Dame, an MBA from the University of Connecticut and his PhD in marketing from Georgia State University.

In addition to being president of Assessment Business Center, a company that offers online, 360º assessments, Tony is chairman of BrainX.com, a company that created the first Online Learning Mastery System™. He is also a founding partner in The Cyrano Group and Platinum Rule Group-- companies which have successfully combined cutting-edge technology and proven psychology to give salespeople the ability to build and maintain positive relationships with hundreds of clients and prospects.

TONY ALESSANDRA
www.alessandra.com